The Artist's and Craftsman's Guide to
Reducing, Enlarging and Transferring Designs

With 24 Sheets of Translucent Reducing and Enlarging Paper

by
RITA WEISS

Dover Publications, Inc., New York

Published in Canada by General Publishing Company, Ltd., 30 Lesmill
Road, Don Mills, Toronto, Ontario.
Published in the United Kingdom by Constable and Company, Ltd.

*The Artist's and Craftsman's Guide to Reducing, Enlarging and
Transferring Designs* is a new work, first published by Dover Publications, Inc., in 1983.

International Standard Book Number: 0-486-24142-4

Manufactured in the United States of America
Dover Publications, Inc., 180 Varick Street, New York, N.Y. 10014

How to Use This Book

No matter what craft medium one works in, there comes a time when one feels the need to look for new designs. Whether you make wooden plaques, do tole painting, embroider tablecloths or hook rugs, eventually the urge to leave the pre-drawn, pre-digested kits and to strike out on your own will arise. For the relatively few people gifted with a certain amount of drawing ability, this becomes a simple task, but for most of us, who express ourselves creatively in other ways, the problem emerges of how to go about, first, finding a suitable design; secondly, reducing or enlarging it to the proper size; and thirdly, transferring it to the chosen medium.

You can learn to solve all these problems by following these simple instructions and by using the handy Reducing and Enlarging Paper in this book. You need not be a designer or an artist to create designs for your craft projects; to be successful, you need only have the desire to produce a finished project that will be yours alone.

CREATIVE DESIGN
WITH READY-MADE MOTIFS

Since there is almost nothing that cannot be used as a motif for a craft project, the sources of design possibilities are limitless. In your own home you can find dozens of motifs just in your wallpaper, draperies and upholstery. Take a design from your favorite china plate and make a beautiful wooden plaque. Because of their simplicity, the illustrations in children's schoolbooks and coloring books translate into ideal rug-hooking projects. Greeting cards and calendar art provide interesting designs, as do book covers, posters and magazine advertisements. The simple, bright colors of the Sunday comics can make interesting and simple stuffed toys. A child's drawing takes on a new dimension when it is fired onto a ceramic plate.

If you enjoy doing research, there are countless books with designs in them. In fact, Dover Publications issues a whole series of inexpensive Pictorial Archive books with hundreds of designs and drawings in many styles and from many countries. You can buy them at your local bookstore or order them by mail from the publisher. To get a free Pictorial Archive catalog (which also has dozens of good, useable pictures in it, by the way), send a postcard to Dover Publications, Inc., 180 Varick Street, New York, N.Y. 10014.

Once you have selected a motif, you need only concern yourself with a few basic design considerations: whether or not to combine it with other motifs and perhaps a border (and if so how to organize these elements); and working out an attractive color scheme. The principles of good design have been covered rather extensively in many books on the subject, so a visit to your local bookstore or library should expose you to a variety of good books ranging from the very elementary and practical to the advanced and highly theoretical. The following hints will help you to avoid common pitfalls and familiarize you with some of the basics peculiar to designing for craft projects.

1. **Unity.** Remember the useful maxim, "Less is more." Be careful not to include too much in one project. For example, if you are using a good, strong design such as the Empire State Building, don't weaken it by adding extraneous stars, portraits of former mayors, scenes of New York, etc. And if, after careful thought, you do add other elements, make sure that they are subordinate to the principal motif.

2. **Scale.** The enlargement or reduction of a design will change its impact. An eye rendered at natural size is just another eye, but enlarge it ten times and it becomes a compelling and unusual design.

3. **Pattern and Rhythm.** Pattern and rhythm are achieved through the repetition of the same motif, the same lines and/or the same colors. Pattern and rhythm are often automatically achieved in many needlework projects because of the regularized character of evenweave fabrics.

4. **Contrast.** Despite the need for unity, every work of art must have some strong points of contrast or it will be lifeless and boring. Every artist strives for a delicate balance between unity and contrast.

When you select a design to copy or adapt, you are exercising a sophisticated judgment. There is creativity in the discovery of the beauty in a cigar label, a cartoon, a gravestone or even a manhole cover. All art begins with discovery, fresh visual perception. The world offers endless possibilities to the painter, the photographer and the craft designer. Each artist first selects an image and then adapts it to his medium. The adaptation can be minimal if the discovery and perception are fresh and shrewd. View everything as a possible design idea for a craft project; extreme adaptation is not essential to creativity.

If the design that you wish to work with is from a source that is not easily handled—for instance, a large piece of material, mounted wallpaper, a drawing from a rare book or your favorite china plate—it is a good idea to work with a tracing. To prepare a tracing, take a sheet of regular tracing paper (not one of the sheets of special paper in this book) and pin or tape it to the area you wish to copy. Now trace the design onto the tracing paper and work from the tracing, reducing or enlarging it and transferring it according to the following instructions.

DETERMINING THE CORRECT DESIGN SIZE FOR YOUR PROJECT

Before beginning to work on any project, determine the optimum size for the design you plan to use. If you have a piece of fabric that measures 6″ x 8″, you don't want to find yourself trying to transfer a design onto it which is 6″ x 9″ or 7″ x 8″.

All the dimensions of a design reduce and/or enlarge in proportion to one another. That is, if you double the size of a design, both the width and the height increase at the same ratio. If you have a design which is 6″ wide by 9″ high, and you wish to make it 8″ wide, the height will also be enlarged proportionately. If you remember your basic high-school mathematics you will realize that the original 6″ width is being enlarged by one-third (2 inches) to give you the new 8″ width; therefore the 9″ height will also be enlarged by one-third (3 inches) to give you the new height of 12″. However, if mathematics was never your forte, you may find dealing with thirds, quarters and other ratios difficult to perceive, let alone using them to calculate size changes in designs that don't measure in nice, neat round numbers. Fortunately, there are several easy nonmathematical methods of determining proportions that are commonly used by professional artists, photographers and printers.

The Proportion Wheel

One of the easiest is to use a proportion wheel, a handy device that not only determines the new length and width of a design but also calculates the percentage of reduction or enlargement as well. A proportion wheel is a very handy tool for any craftsperson, and it is a simple one to make and use. On Plates A and B (pages 13 & 15) you will find the necessary special parts for making your own proportion wheel.

Cut Plates A and B out of this book and carefully glue them to pieces of thin cardboard, such as shirt cardboard. Next, carefully cut out both circles. Cut out the "window" in the smaller circle, and then with a thin, sharp instrument, such as a needle, make a hole in the center of both circles exactly where indicated. Place the smaller circle on top of the larger circle and join the two circles through the center holes with a paper fastener. The smaller circle can now be made to rotate over the larger one.

The scale on the smaller circle indicates the *original size* of your design, and the larger circle indicates the new (larger or smaller) size. The "window" tells you what percentage of the original size your new pattern will be. Test your proportion wheel by placing the 6″ mark on the smaller circle directly under the 6″ mark on the larger wheel. Note that all the other numbers on both scales also align and that the window shows the percentage of original size to be 100, which means that you have neither reduced nor enlarged the design. If the numbers do not line up, you do not have your paper fastener in the exact center of both circles. Remove the fastener and replace it correctly.

Now let us see how easy it is to figure out the proportions discussed above. Let's say you have a design that measures 6″ wide by 9″ high, and that you want to enlarge it so that it becomes 8″ wide. You need to find out what the new height will be. Move the 6″ mark on the smaller circle (the original width) so that it aligns with the 8″ mark on the larger circle (the desired new width). Holding the wheel in place, check the 9″ mark on the smaller circle. You will find that it aligns with the 12″ mark on the larger circle, which tells you that if you increase the width to 8″, the height will become 12″; the window tells you that the new size is 133% of (or ⅓ larger than) the original size. Similarly, by moving the 6″ mark on the smaller wheel to align with the 7″ mark on the larger one, you find that at this enlargement (about 116% of original size), the new height will be about 10½″.

Get used to working with the proportion wheel by trying out a few more sample enlargements and reductions. Say you have a design that measures 3¾″ wide by 5″ high, and that you want to bring the height up to 7″. Align the 5″ mark on the smaller wheel with the 7″ mark on the larger one. Then see what aligns with the 3¾″ mark on the smaller wheel. You'll find that it's 5¼″—the new width—and the "window" will show that the enlargement is to 140% of original size (in other words, 40% larger).

Reductions work exactly the same as enlargements. A design that measures 8″ x 10″ comes down to 6¼″ by about 7¹³⁄₁₆″ when reduced to 78% of original size.

There will be times when the measurements on the smaller circle will fall between two markings on the larger circle. Professional printers and engravers figure their enlargements and reductions in very small fractions (even as low as ¹⁄₆₄″), but for most craft projects your results will be satisfactory if you deal in sixteenths or even eighths of an inch.

The Diagonal-Line Method

Scale drawings are another method used by commercial artists for determining the new size of a drawing which is to be reduced or enlarged. This is also a simple method and has the advantage of giving you an indication of the overall size of your finished design. Let us start with a 3⅜″ wide x 5″ high design which we are going to enlarge to 5¼″ wide. We haven't yet determined the new height of this design, and we are also interested in seeing whether the new proportions will not only fit on the material we are going to use, but also will look pleasing on it.

Take a piece of tracing paper and lay it over the original design. Now enclose the original motif in a rectangle which is 3⅜″ x 5″ (*Figure 1*). Be careful to make all corners right angles; use a T-square or else draw on transparent graph paper. Letter the corners *A, B, C* and *D* as in the figure. Extend line *CD* to the desired 5¼″ width; designate this point *X*. Draw line *XY*, which can be any height, but must be parallel to line *CA*. Draw a diagonal line from *C* through *B* to where it intersects the *XY* line. The point *Z* at which the diagonal line crosses *XY* shows the new height of the drawing (7¾″). Extend the other two lines to make a new rectangle which will be the overall size of the new drawing.

To reduce a drawing, draw a rectangle the size of the original design as *ABCD* in Figure 2. Draw a diagonal line from *C* to *B*. Measure the desired new width from *C* to *X* and draw line *XY* parallel to *CA* and *DB*. Mark point *Z* where the diagonal line intersects line *XY*. Draw a line from *Z* to *CA* to get the new rectangle.

REDUCING AND ENLARGING METHODS

After using the proportion wheel or the diagonal-line method to determine that the new proportions of your design will fit and look well on the material you are planning to use, you are ready to prepare an exact copy of the motif to the correct size. There are a number of simple methods for doing this.

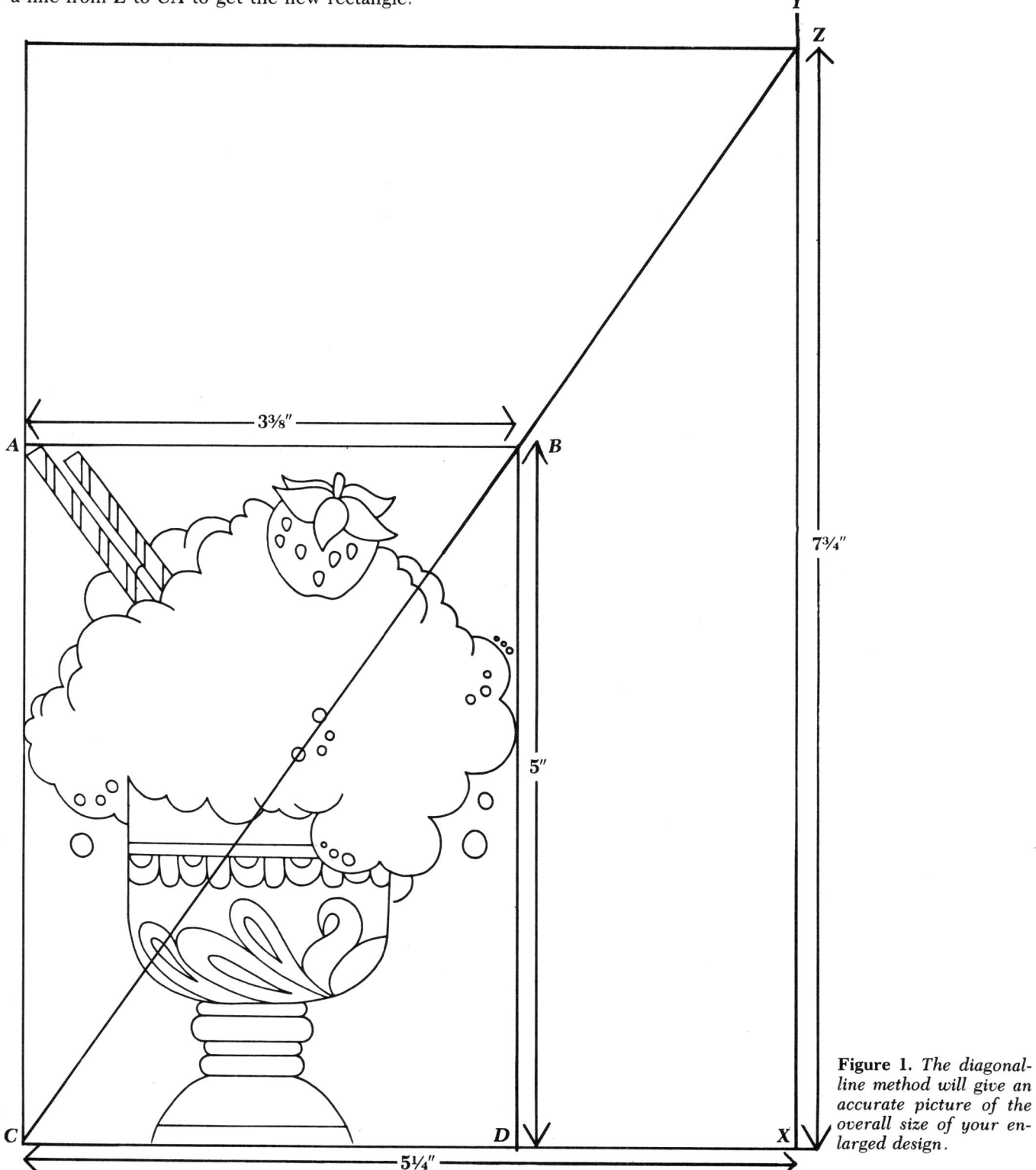

Figure 1. *The diagonal-line method will give an accurate picture of the overall size of your enlarged design.*

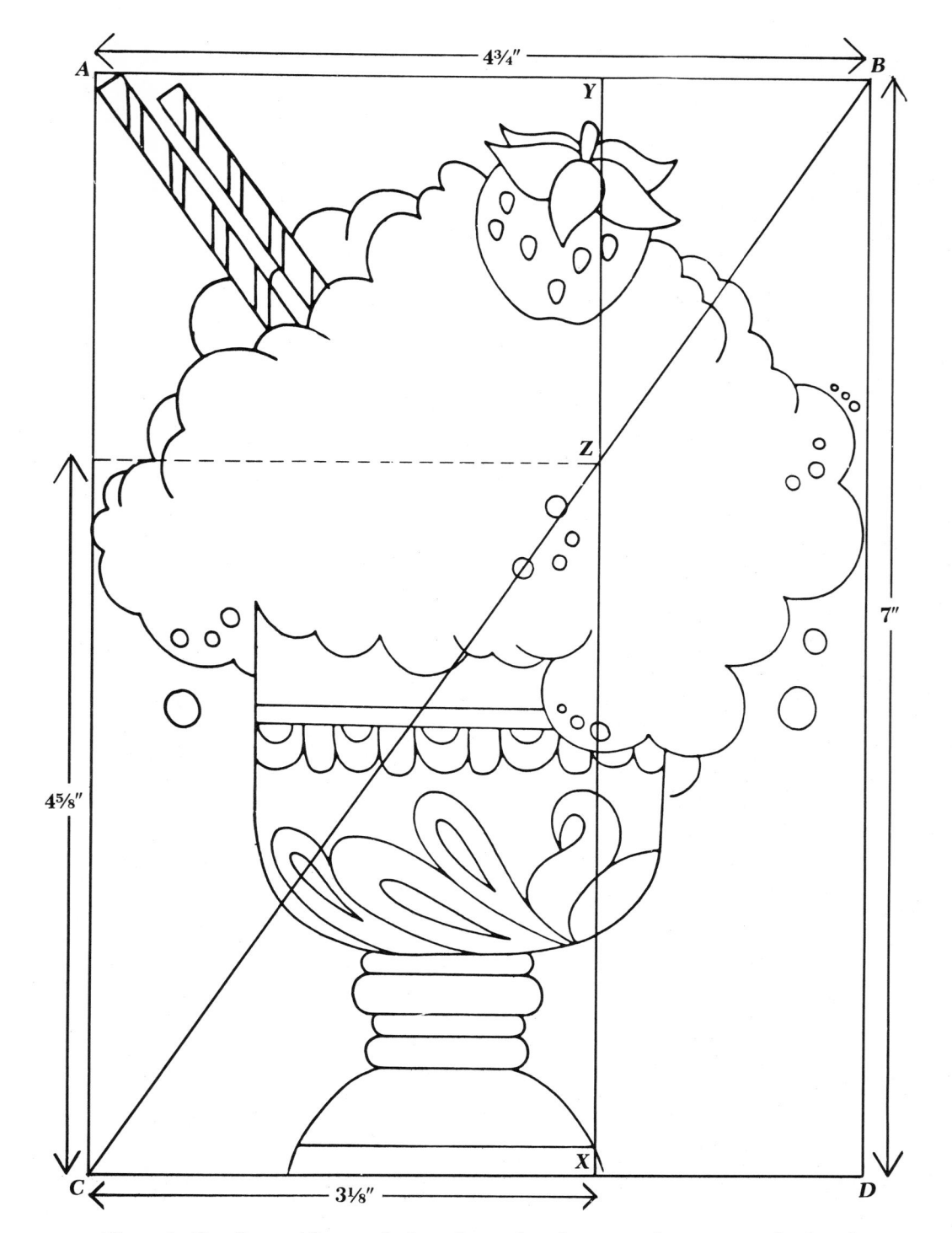

Figure 2. *The diagonal-line method can be used to determine the new size of reduced as well as enlarged artwork.*

Photographic Methods

The easiest way to get an enlarged or reduced copy of a design is by photography. While this method has the advantage of allowing you to get your design reproduced to an *exact* size, it can be costly unless you possess your own photographic equipment. In addition there is the often annoying lapse of time between deciding upon a design and having it processed.

A photograph may be required if you wish to enlarge or reduce a black-and-white design that also has gray tones or a color photograph where the shading is an essential part of your design idea. Ask for a continuous tone matte print. If your original is in color, the results will not be an exact duplicate, but the design elements will be clear enough for most craft projects. You can get an 8″x10″ continuous tone print made for about $9.00. If you are working from a photograph and have the original

6

negative, it will be cheaper to use it to prepare the enlarged or reduced print.

If your artwork is black and white without any shading (tones of gray), a line stat may be all that you will need. Many typesetters and printers have photostat equipment, and they may be willing to enlarge or reduce your design for you for a nominal fee. You can also have such designs copied inexpensively by a professional photo-copying service that has duplicating equipment that can enlarge and reduce. You can locate such companies in the Yellow Pages of your telephone book under "Photo Copying."

You can also enlarge or reduce a design by means of a 35mm slide. Attach a piece of white paper to a wall (not to a screen). Using a slide projector, project your slide onto the white paper. If you move the projector closer to the white paper, the image will get smaller; if you move the projector farther away, the image will grow larger. When the image is the desired size, trace your design onto the white paper. You may have to move around quite a bit to keep your body from interfering with the light source.

The Pantograph

The pantograph *(Figure 3)* is one of the oldest tools for reducing and enlarging designs. Basically the instrument consists of two sets of arms which are linked together. A pointer pin is attached where one set of arms join. To enlarge a design, one end of the other set of arms is anchored securely; the other end is fitted with a pencil. When the pointer traces the outlines of the original design, the pencil produces a copy up to twice the size of the original, the size depending on the length and spread of the arms. If you wish to reduce the design (down to half size), you simply reverse the positions of the pointer and the pencil.

Although pantographs are no longer widely available, you may be able to purchase one at a large art-supply store. If you are at all handy with tools you can construct a simple pantograph that will prepare half-size and double-size copies. Make the arms out of at least 1″ wide hardwood stock. The two long arms are equal in length and the two short arms are half as long. Drill holes into the pivot points and insert 1½″ threaded bolts with nuts. The pointer can be a pushpin or a small nail.

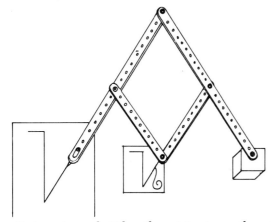

Figure 3. *A pantograph. When the pointer traces the original artwork (center), the pencil makes an enlarged copy of it (left).*

Square-Grid Method Using Reducing and Enlarging Paper

The technique used most often by craft workers is the square-grid method. If you have been working projects from patterns in craft books and magazines, you are probably already familiar with this method. To enlarge the pattern, the design is first traced onto a grid and then copied square for square onto a larger grid. To reduce a design, you copy it onto a smaller grid.

In the center of the book are 24 sheets of translucent Reducing and Enlarging Paper. The No. 1 sheets have ¼″ squares printed in light lines. The No. 2 sheets have, in addition to the light ¼″ squares, bold lines indicating ½″ squares. This paper is to be used to enlarge a design traced on No. 1 paper to *twice* original size (200%). The No. 3 sheets, with bold lines marking off ¾″ squares, are to be used to enlarge a design traced on No. 1 paper to *three times* original size (300%). The No. 4 paper, with 1″ squares marked off by bold lines, is used to enlarge a design traced on No. 1 paper to *four times* original size (400%).

Unless the design you want to enlarge is already printed on a grid, as designs in crafts and hobby magazines frequently are, this is how you begin. Remove a sheet of No. 1 Reducing and Enlarging Paper from the book. Lay the art work to be copied onto a flat surface and place the upper left-hand corner of the sheet of special paper over the pattern that you wish to enlarge. Tape down the edges to prevent the design and the paper from slipping. Try to line up any horizontal or vertical lines in the artwork with the horizontal or vertical lines on the paper. You won't be able to do this for all of the lines, but you will find it helpful to get some of the main horizontals or verticals aligned. Now, completely ignoring the squares on the Reducing and Enlarging Paper, trace the design onto it.

Professional graphic artists use a light box when tracing. This is a device consisting of a glass-topped table with a strong light beneath the glass. You can build a very simple light box by taping together all of the sides of a cardboard box except the top. Over the open side, place a piece of glass, such as that found in a picture frame. (A frosted glass works best.) Put the light inside the box and let it shine below the glass. Don't use too strong a bulb as the glass can get hot and you can sustain quite a burn. If you line the cardboard box with aluminum foil, even a small bulb will give you enough light. You can also tape the design and the Reducing and Enlarging Paper to a windowpane and use the light coming through the window as your light source. (The Reducing and Enlarging Paper can be made more translucent by rubbing the sheet with salad oil. Use a soft rag and remove any surplus.)

HOW TO ENLARGE A DESIGN

Measure your tracing and then decide how large you want your final design to be. Choose either a new length or width measurement and then, using your proportion wheel, determine what the percentage of enlargement is going to be. For instance, if the design you traced on your sheet of No. 1 Reducing and Enlarging Paper is 3″ wide, and you want to make it 6″ wide, you will enlarge the drawing to 200% of original size, or twice the size of your original drawing; use a sheet of No. 2 Reducing and Enlarging Paper to accomplish this. If you want to make the design larger, say 9″ wide, use No. 3 Reducing and Enlarging Paper to triple the size of the art. The traced design can be made four times as big by using No. 4 Reducing and Enlarging Paper.

Carefully examine your tracing and decide whether you want to double, triple or quadruple its size. Let's say you decide to make it four times as big. Take a sheet of No. 4 Reducing and Enlarging Paper from the book, lay it on a flat surface and carefully copy all the lines that appear in each of the ¼″ squares of your tracing into the corresponding 1″ squares of the No. 4 Paper (see Figure 4). (Ignore the light ¼″ squares on the No. 4 Paper.) Forgetting about what the whole design looks like, work one square at a time, keeping all relationships exactly the same in both size squares. For instance, if the small square has a line which crosses the right side at a point which is one-third of the way from the bottom, the larger square should have a similar line in the corresponding spot. If one of the ¼″ squares has a particularly intricate design in it, you may want to further subdivide this one square either by drawing diagonal lines or by dividing the ¼″ square into ⅛″ squares. Then copy what appears in each ⅛″ square into the corresponding ¼″ light square. When you are finished transferring the design

square by square, it may be necessary to rework some of the lines on the larger drawing to get even joining lines, but your original 3″-wide drawing will now be 12″ wide.

If you want to *double* the size of your tracing, follow the same instructions but use a sheet of No. 2 Reducing and Enlarging Paper. Use No. 3 Paper to triple the size of your tracing.

If you want to enlarge your traced design beyond 400% of original size, take a sheet of No. 1 Reducing and Enlarging Paper and draw your own bold lines on it as follows:

TO ENLARGE	MAKE THIS SIZE BOLD SQUARE	
500% (5 times)	1¼″ square	= 5 x 5 light squares
600% (6 times)	1½″ square	= 6 x 6 light squares
700% (7 times)	1¾″ square	= 7 x 7 light squares
800% (8 times)	2″ square	= 8 x 8 light squares

HOW TO REDUCE A DESIGN

For most craft projects, the problem is to enlarge rather than reduce a pattern. However, when designs are too large, the craft worker can reduce them using the special paper and the square-grid method.

First, study the artwork and decide how much you want to reduce it. Let's say you want to make it half as big as it is. Trace the design onto a sheet of No. 2 Reducing and Enlarging Paper, and then copy it, square for square, onto No. 1 Paper. To reduce the design to ¼ its original size, trace it on No. 4 Paper and then copy it on No. 1 Paper. To reduce it to ⅓ its original size, trace the design on No. 3 Paper and then copy it on No. 1.

HOW TO TRANSFER A DESIGN TO A CRAFT PROJECT

Now that your design is the proper size, it must be transferred from the sheet of Reducing and Enlarging Paper to your craft medium: fabric, wood, metal, ceramic, plastic, etc. There are several satisfactory methods for doing this and each has its advantages and disadvantages. Some of the methods, although easy to work, leave a permanent line on your project. If all of the lines in the pattern are to be covered with paint or thread, this is not a real problem. Other methods produce a line that washes out, but in the process will bleed into thread. If the project will not be washed or if thread is not used, this method will be satisfactory.

Whichever of the following methods you decide upon should always be practiced prior to using it for a finished project. Transfer the design to a piece of scrap material. If the completed craft project is to be washed in warm water, do this with your sample. If the completed project will only be washed in cold water, try this with your sample. If the project is to be baked in a kiln, see how the heat affects the transfer line. In short, experiment to make certain that once you have finished working on a project, the original transfer line does not run, bleed through or remain as a permanent blob, ruining hours of work.

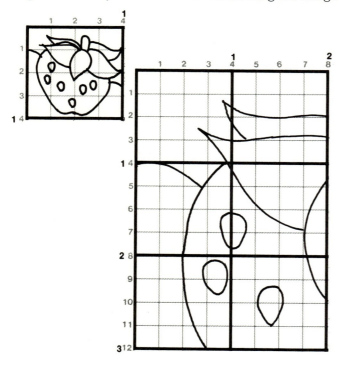

Figure 4. *Copy exactly what appears in each ¼″ square into the corresponding 1″ square (upper left section of enlargement is illustrated).*

Instructions continue after the Reducing and Enlarging Paper

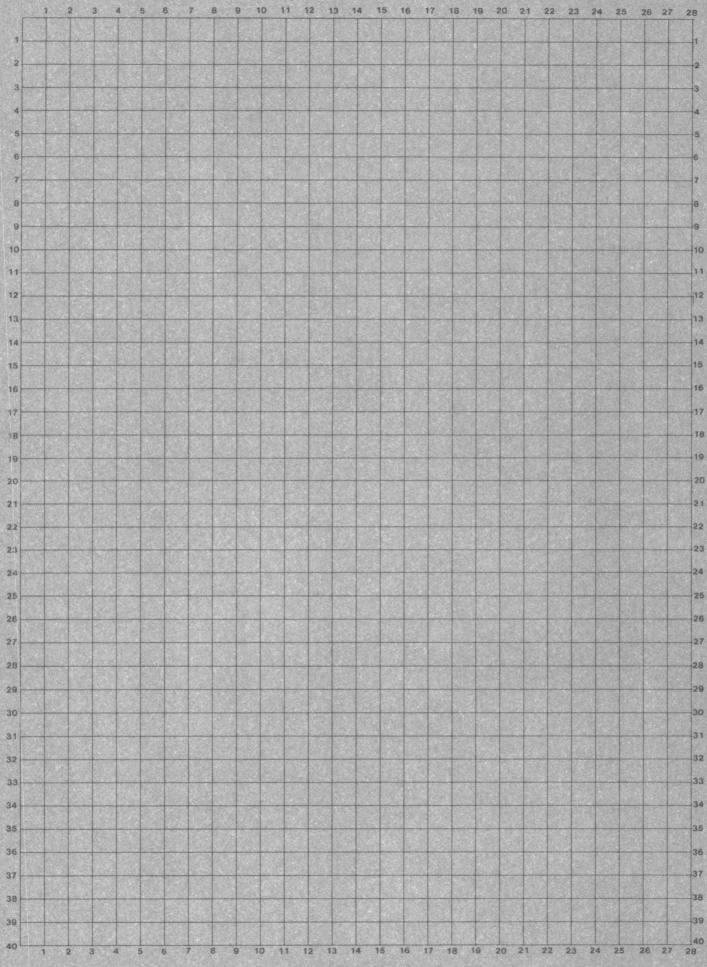

No. 1 Reducing and Enlarging Paper

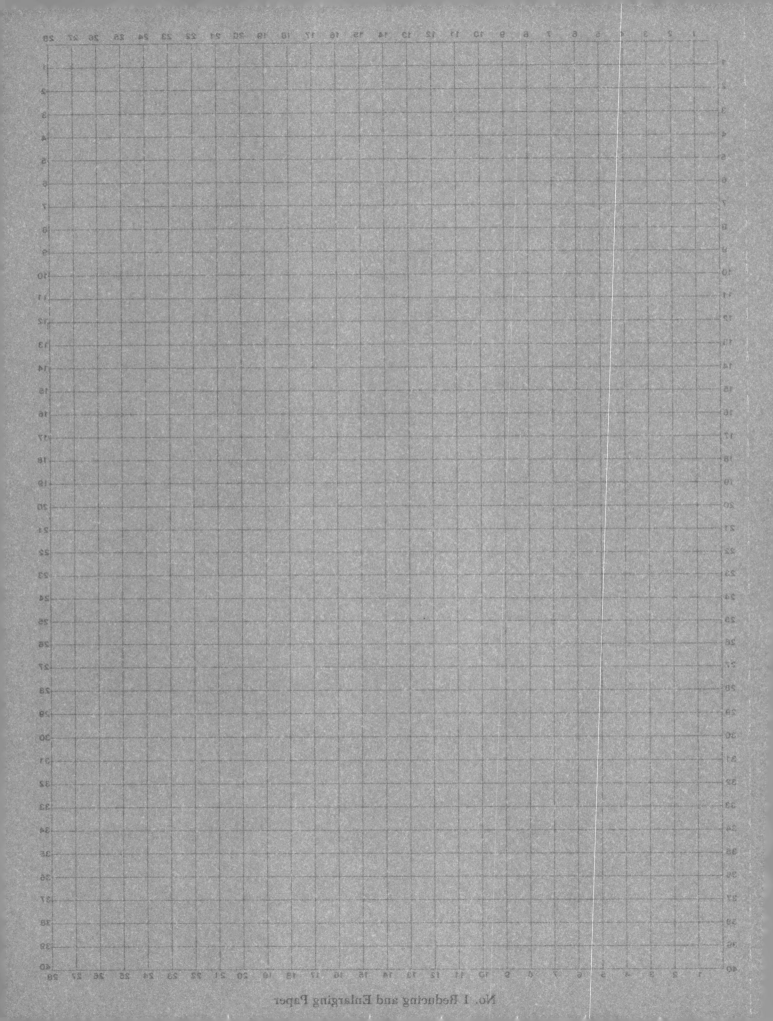

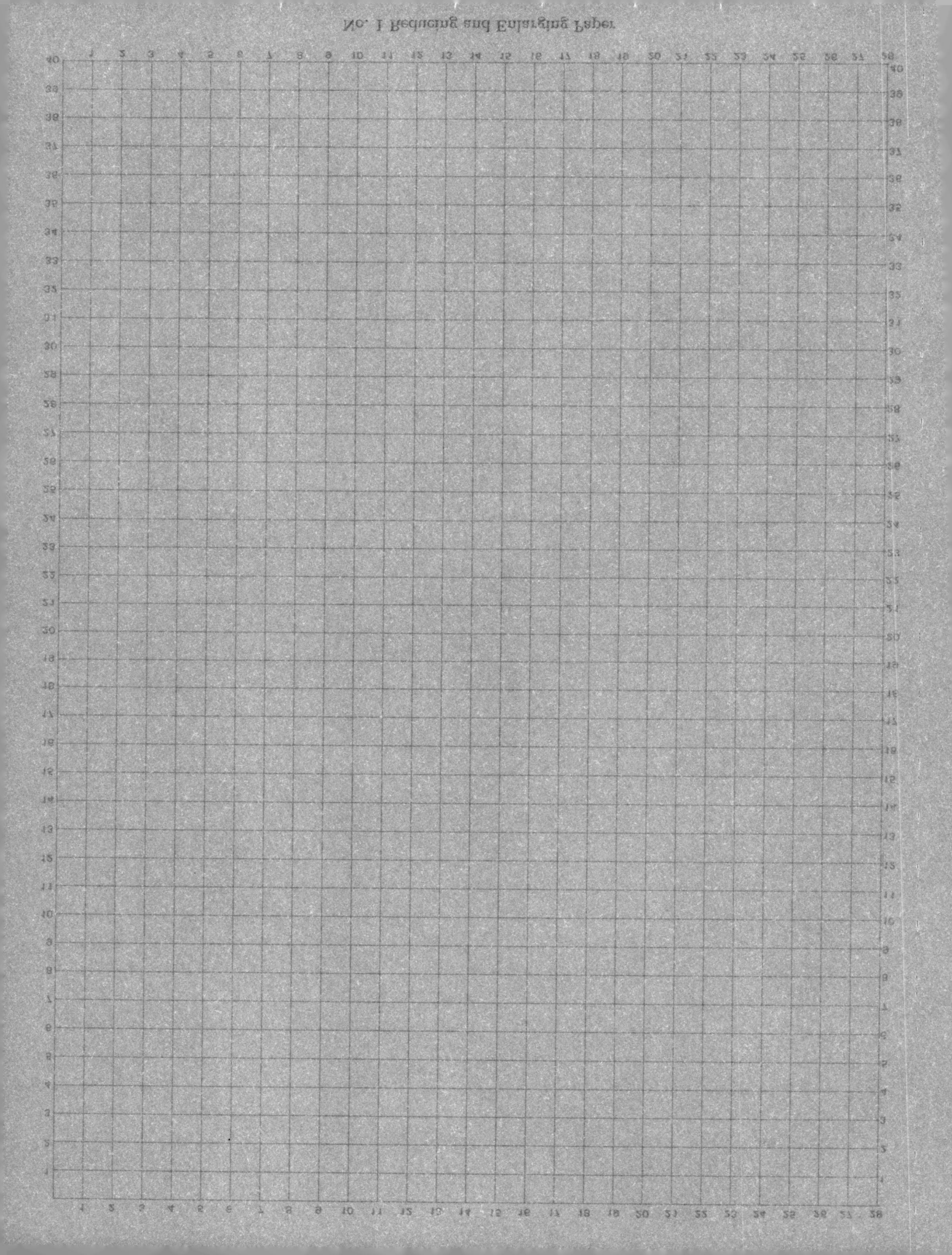

No. 1 Beginning and Estimating Paper

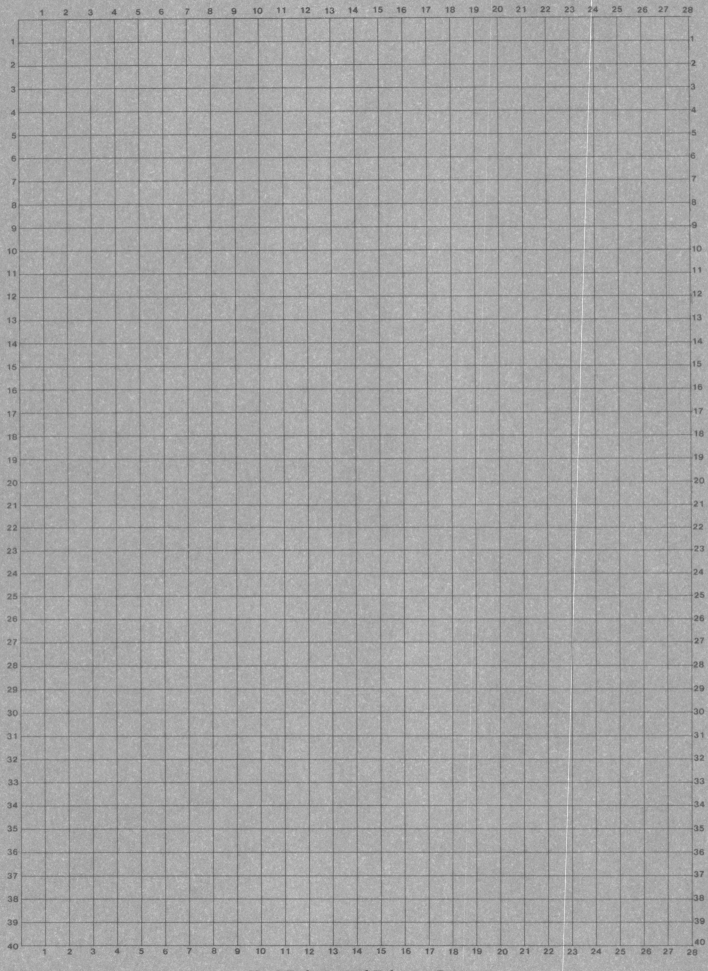

No. 1 Reducing and Enlarging Paper

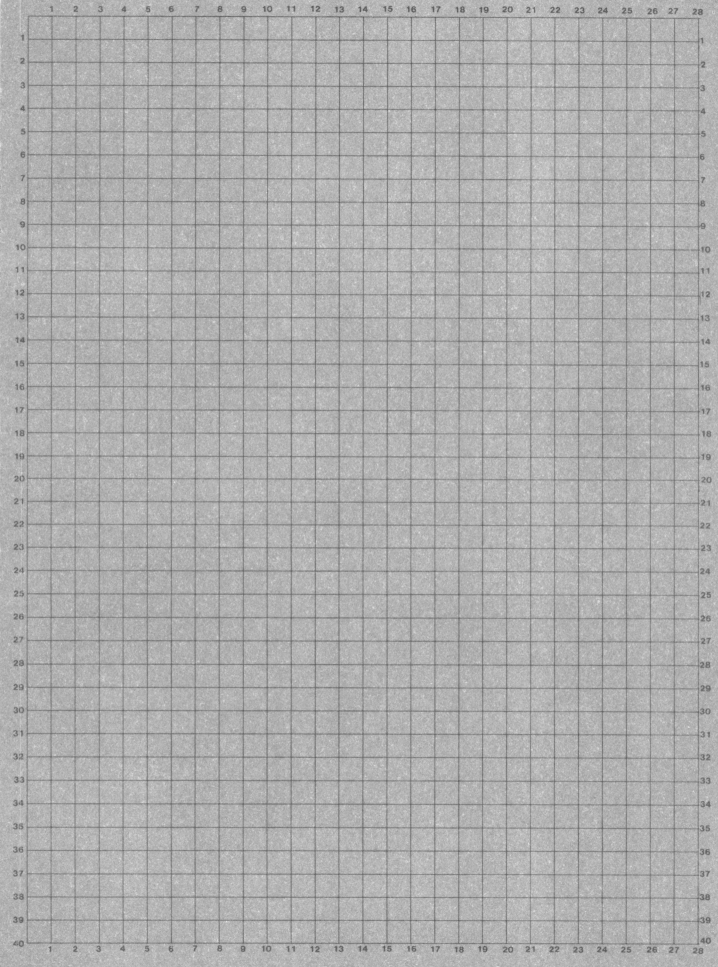

No. 1 Reducing and Enlarging Paper

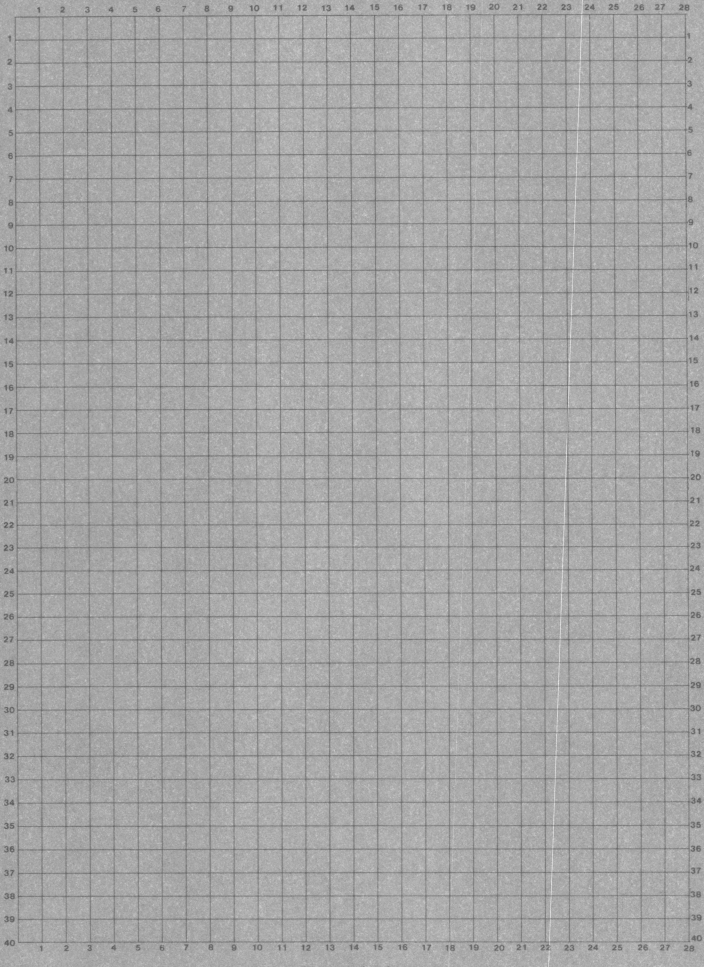

No. 1 Reducing and Enlarging Paper

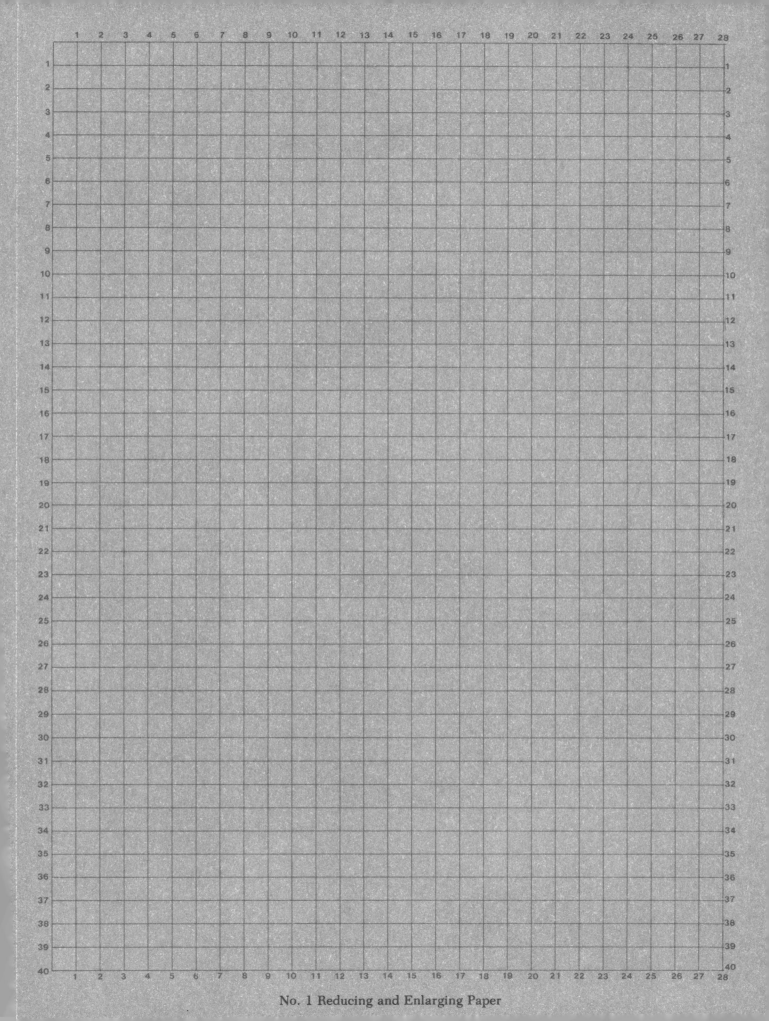

No. 1 Reducing and Enlarging Paper

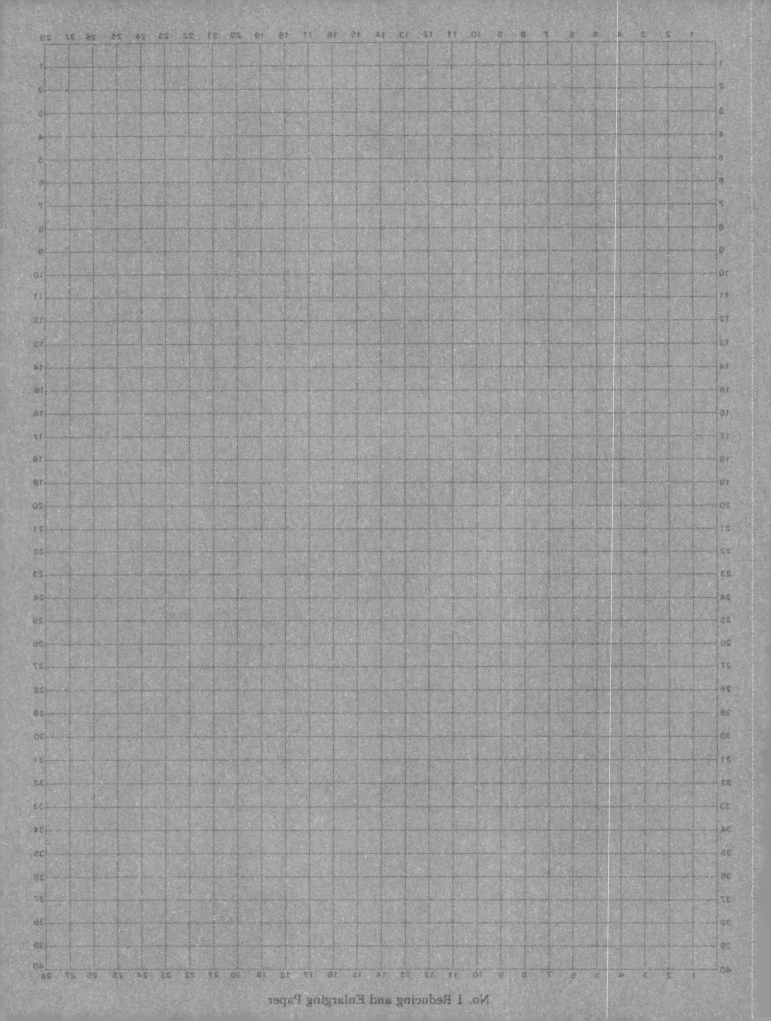

No. 1 Reducing and Enlarging Paper

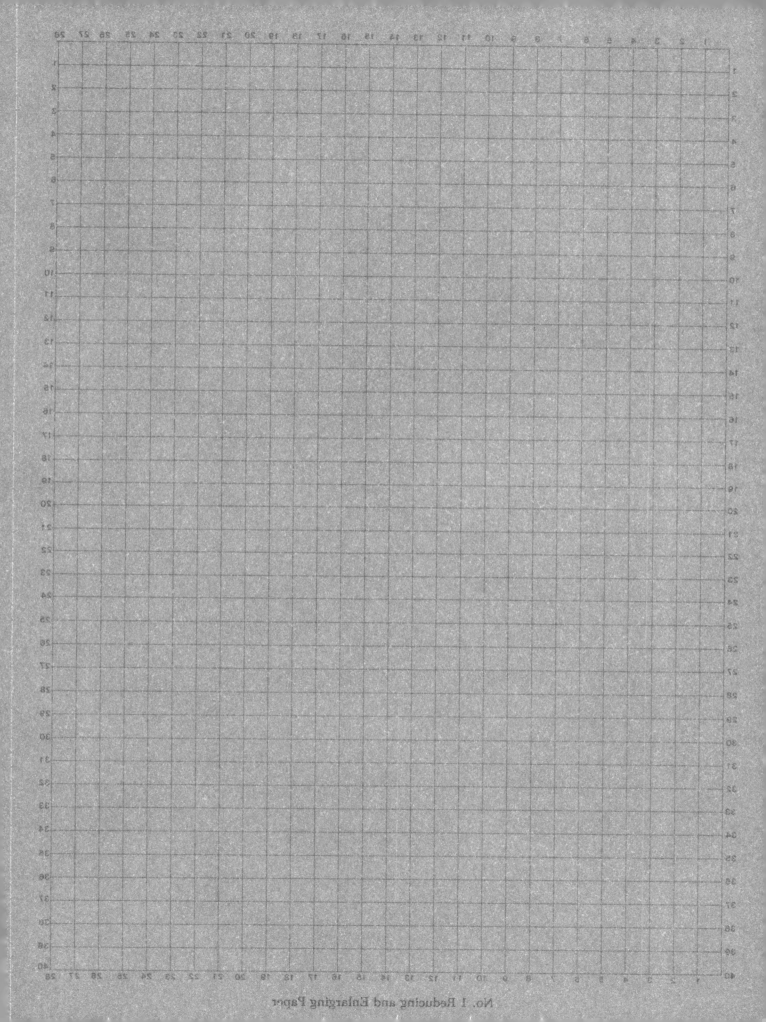

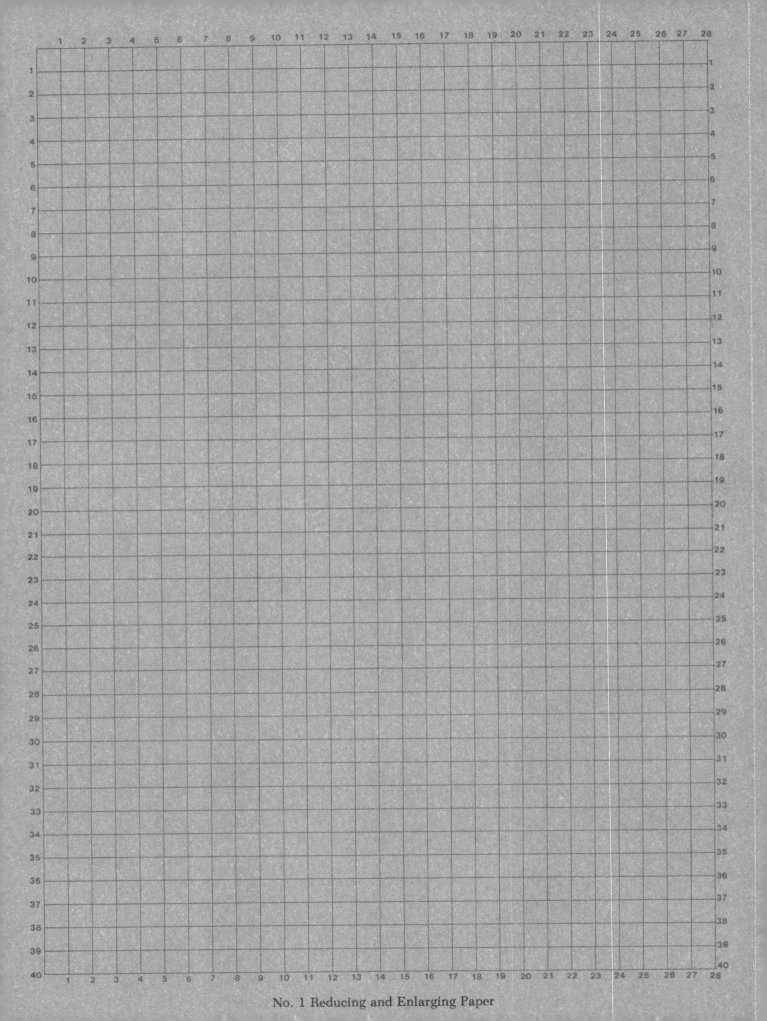

No. 1 Reducing and Enlarging Paper

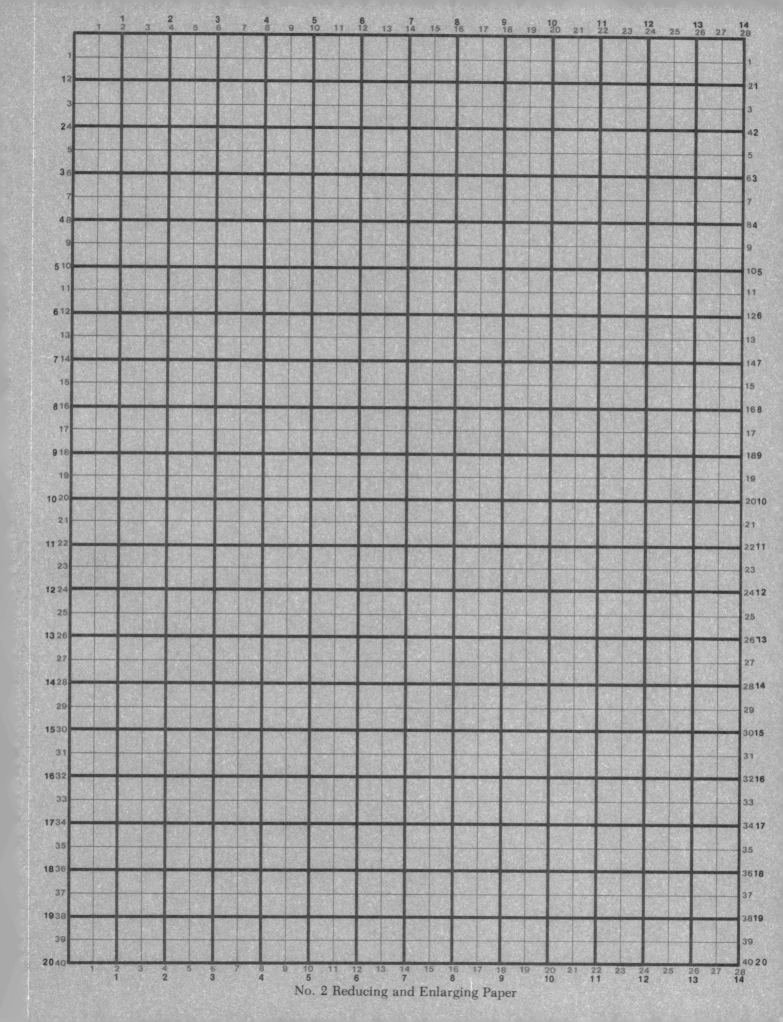

No. 2 Reducing and Enlarging Paper

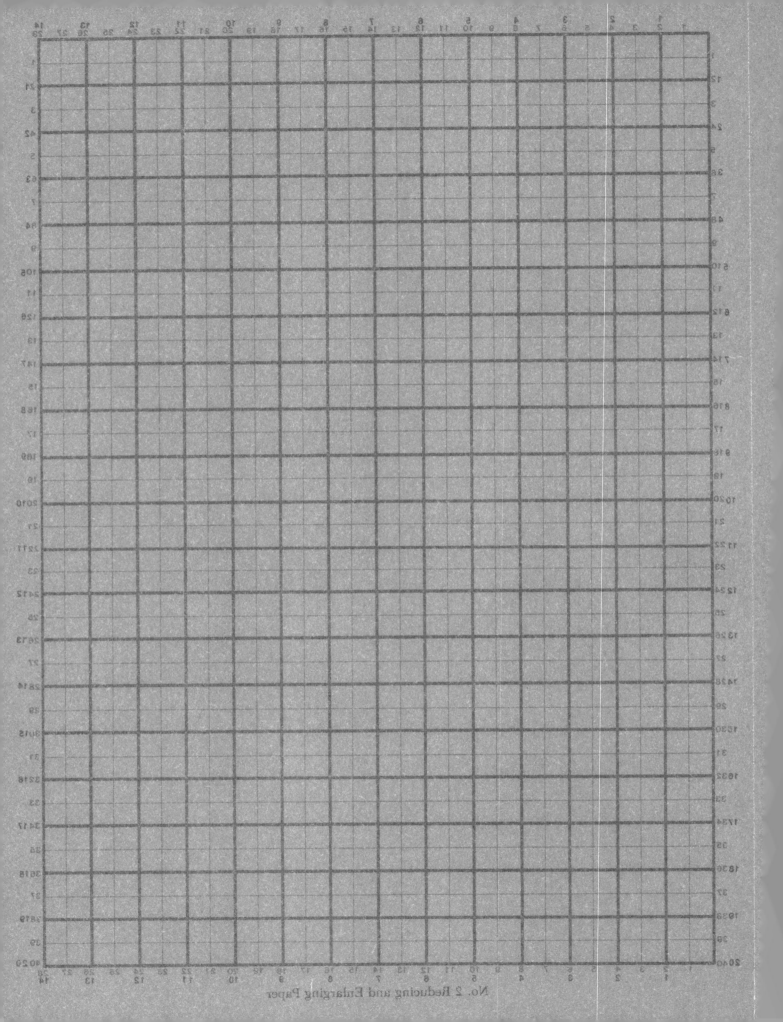

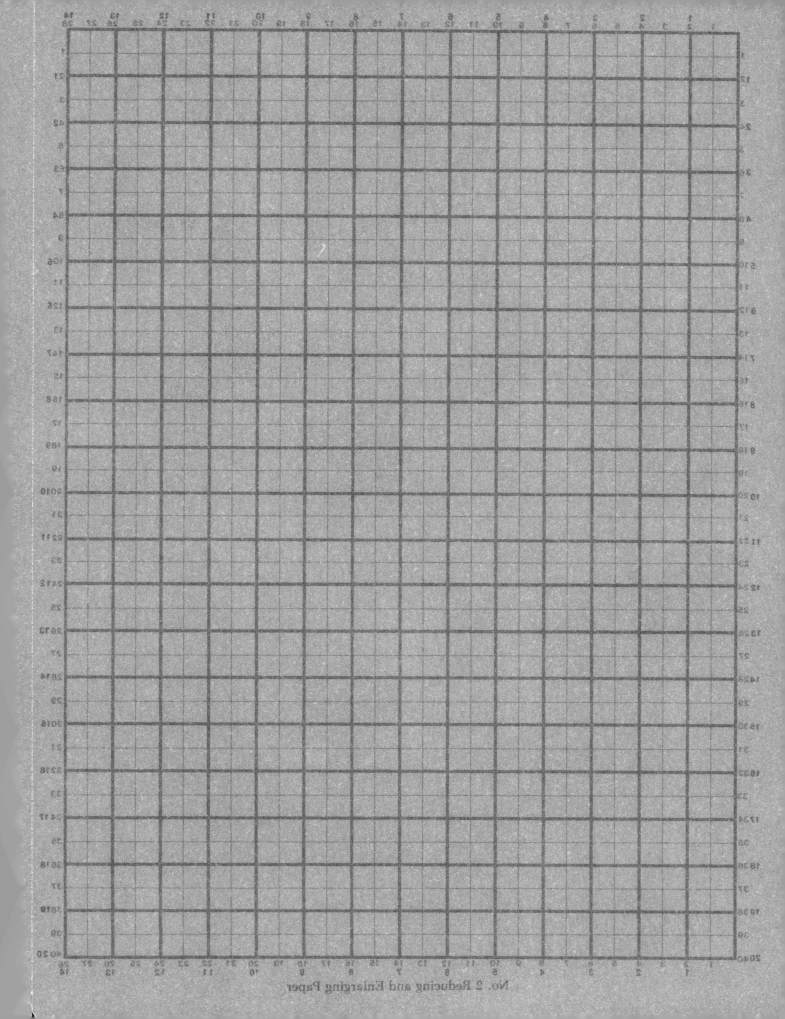

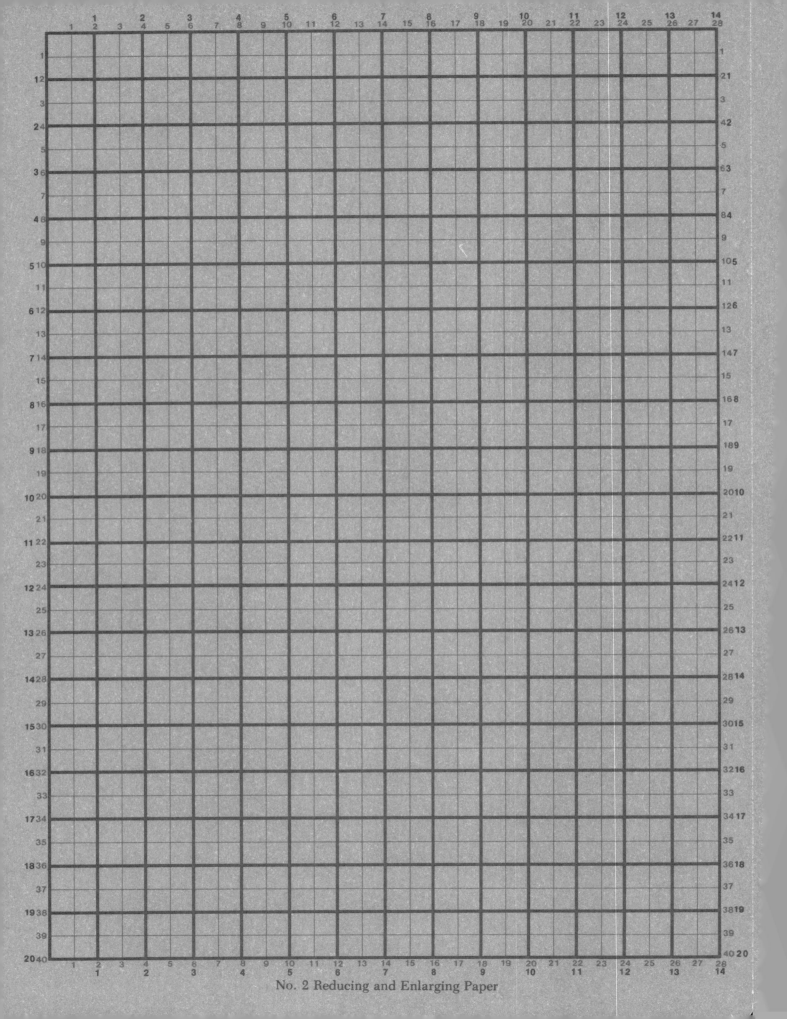

No. 2 Reducing and Enlarging Paper

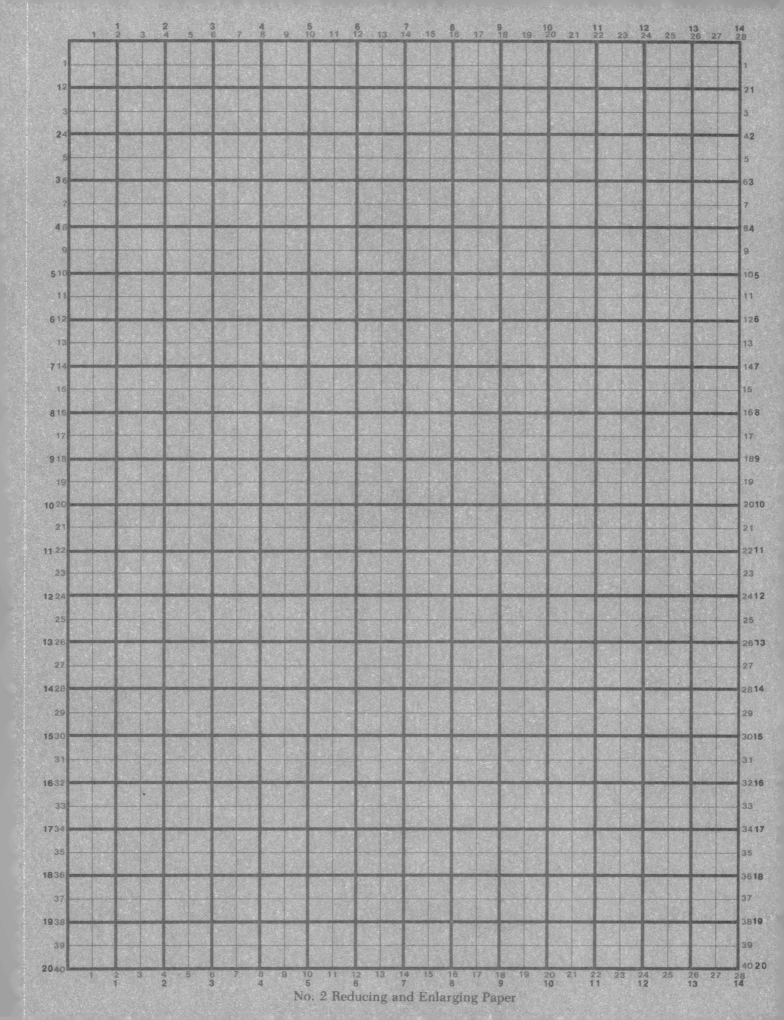

No. 2 Reducing and Enlarging Paper

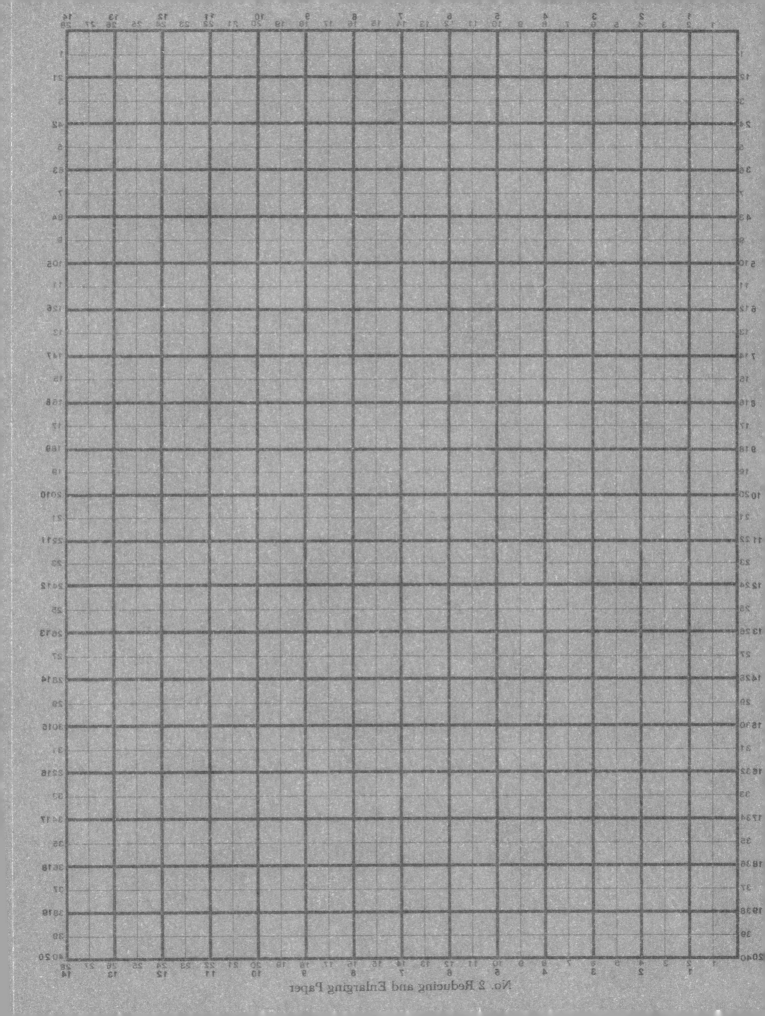

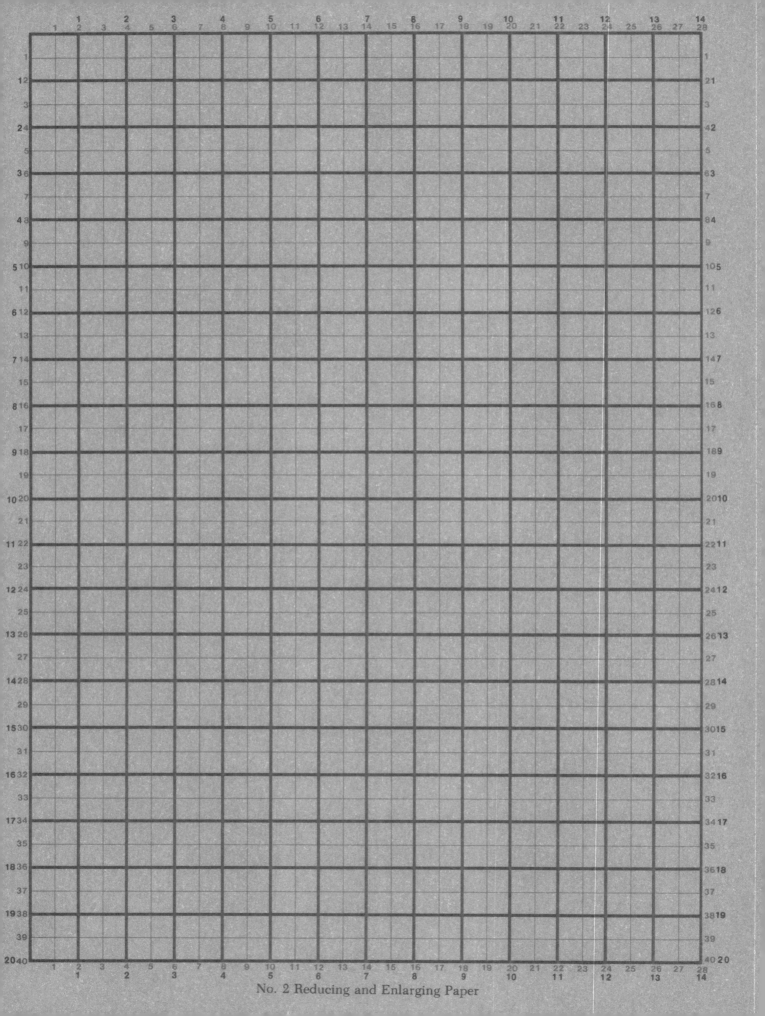

No. 2 Reducing and Enlarging Paper

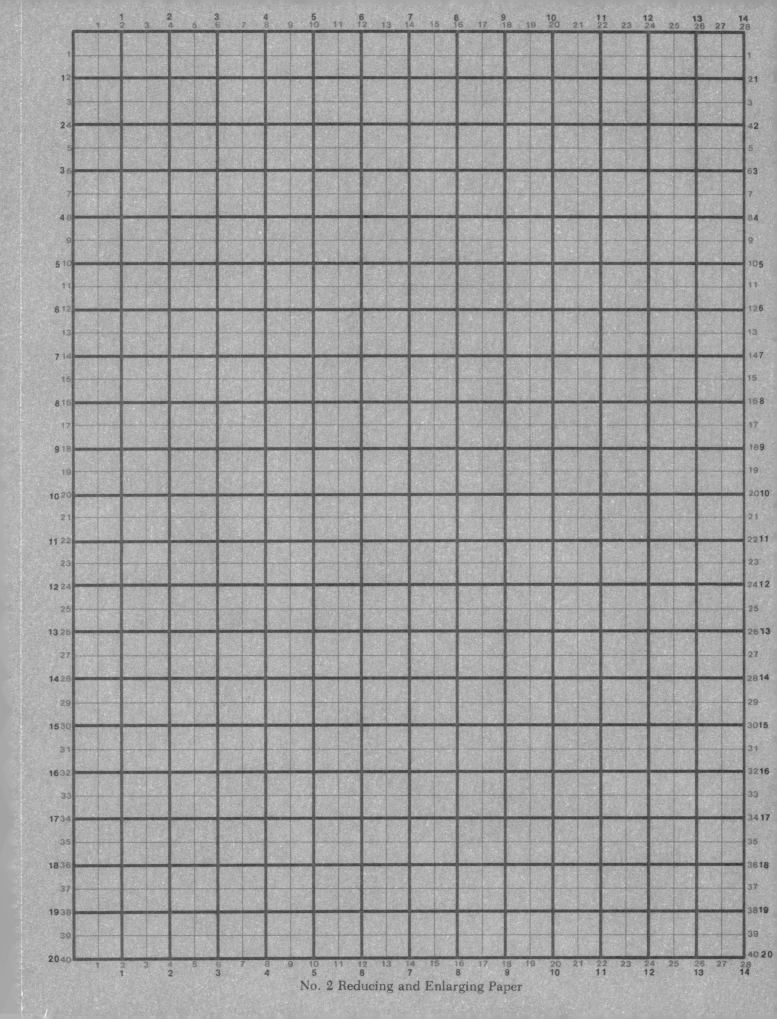

No. 2 Reducing and Enlarging Paper

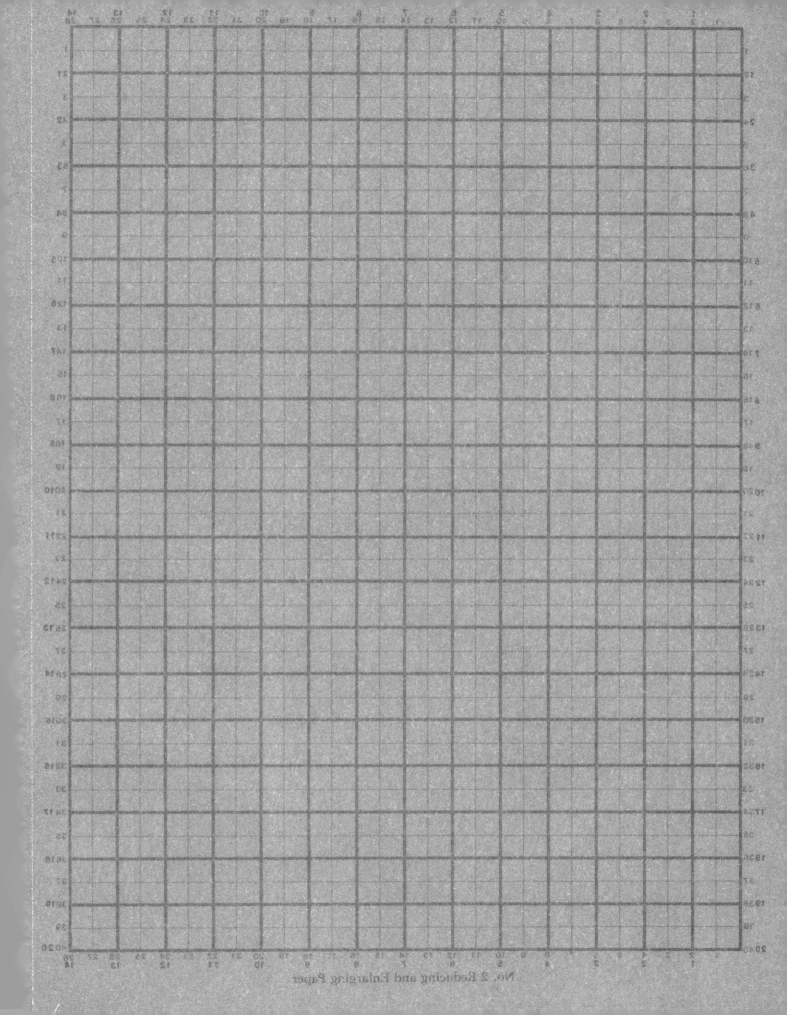

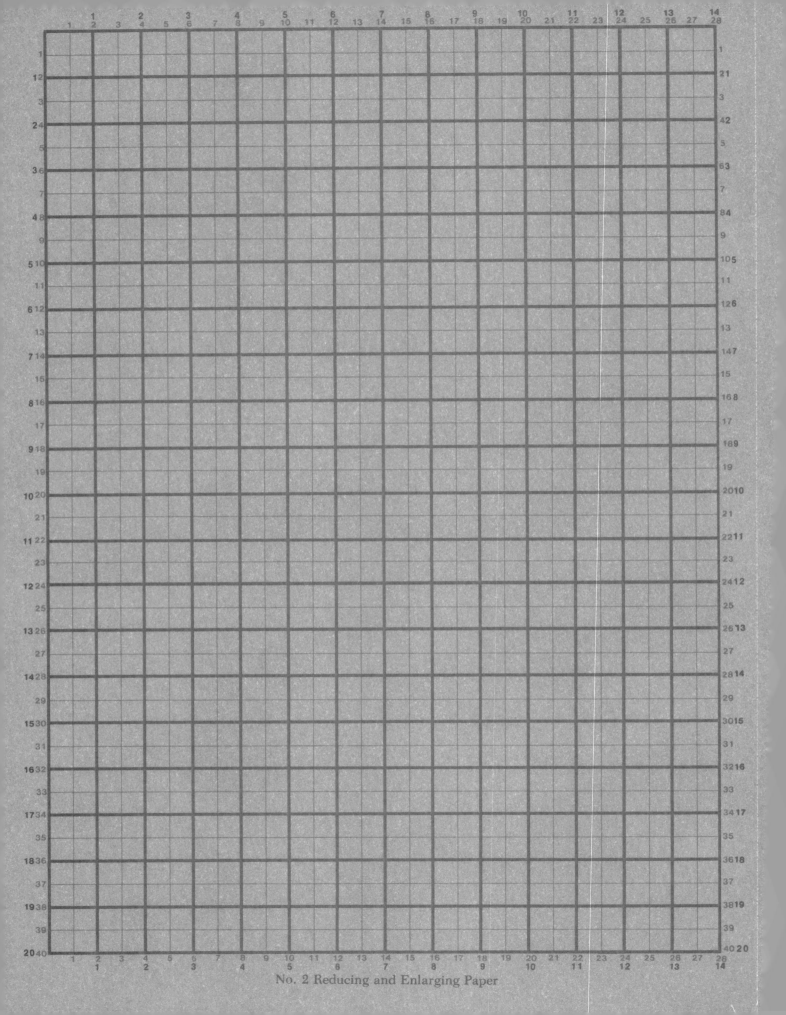

No. 2 Reducing and Enlarging Paper

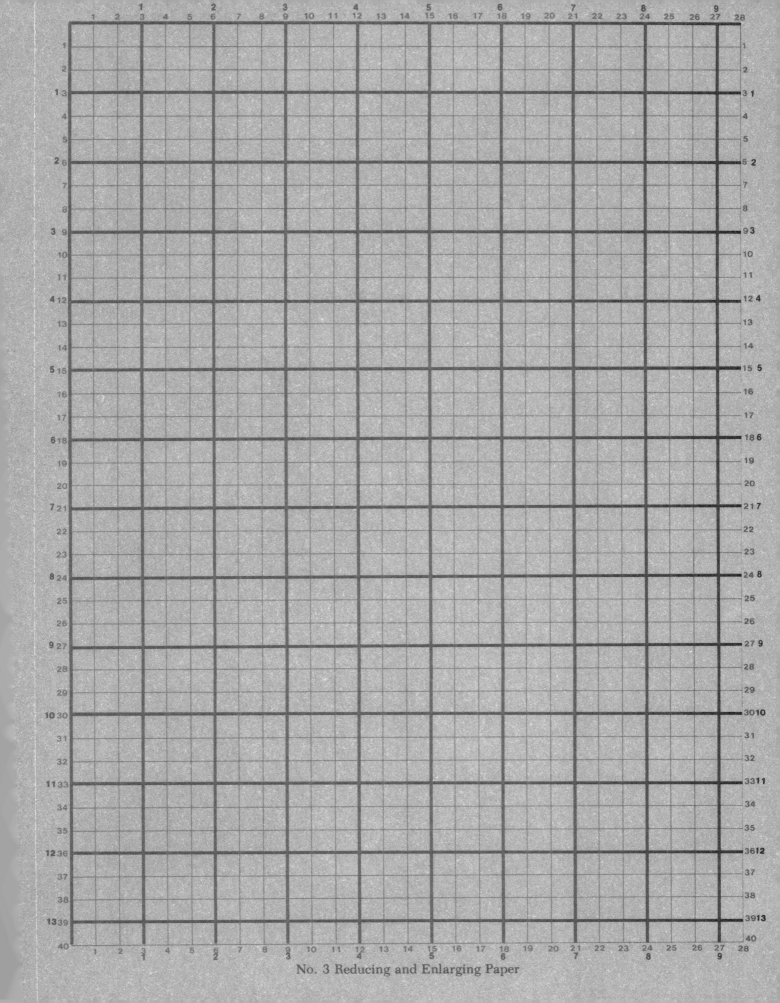

No. 3 Reducing and Enlarging Paper

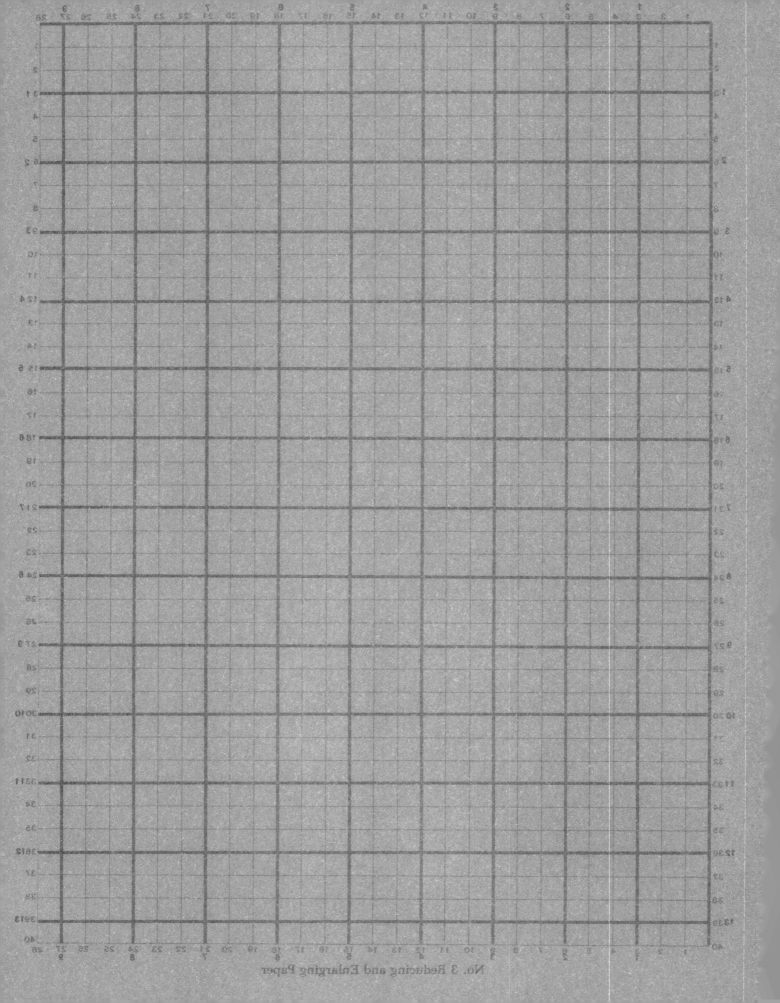

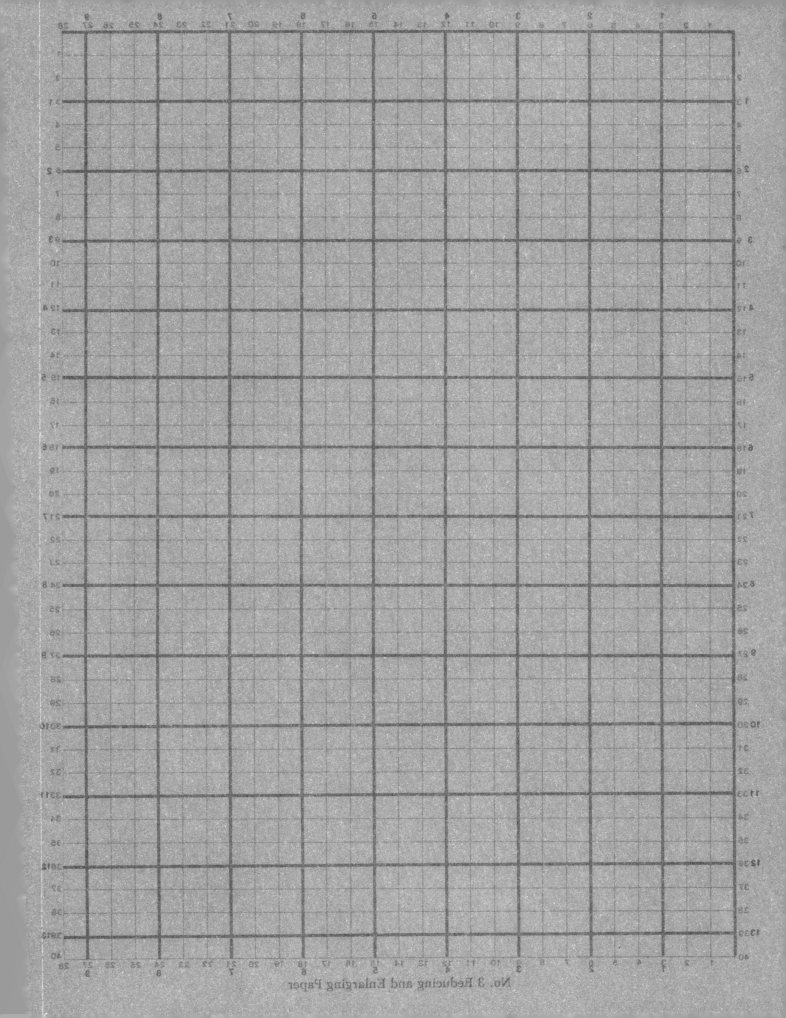

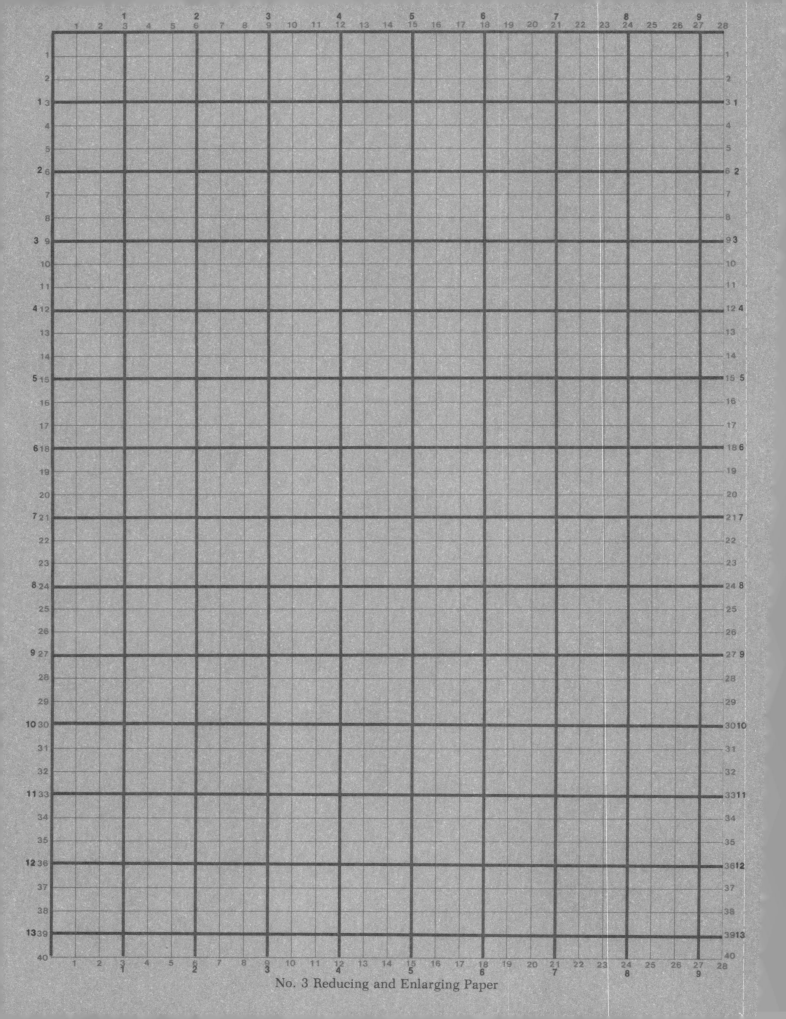

No. 3 Reducing and Enlarging Paper

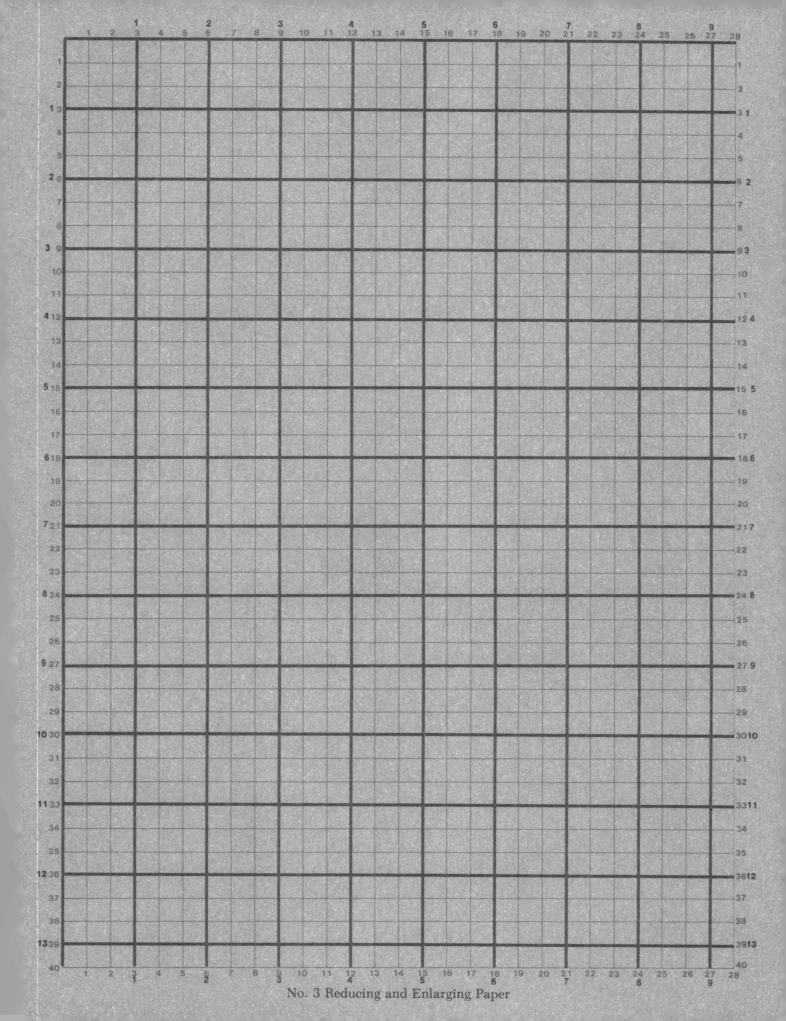

No. 3 Reducing and Enlarging Paper

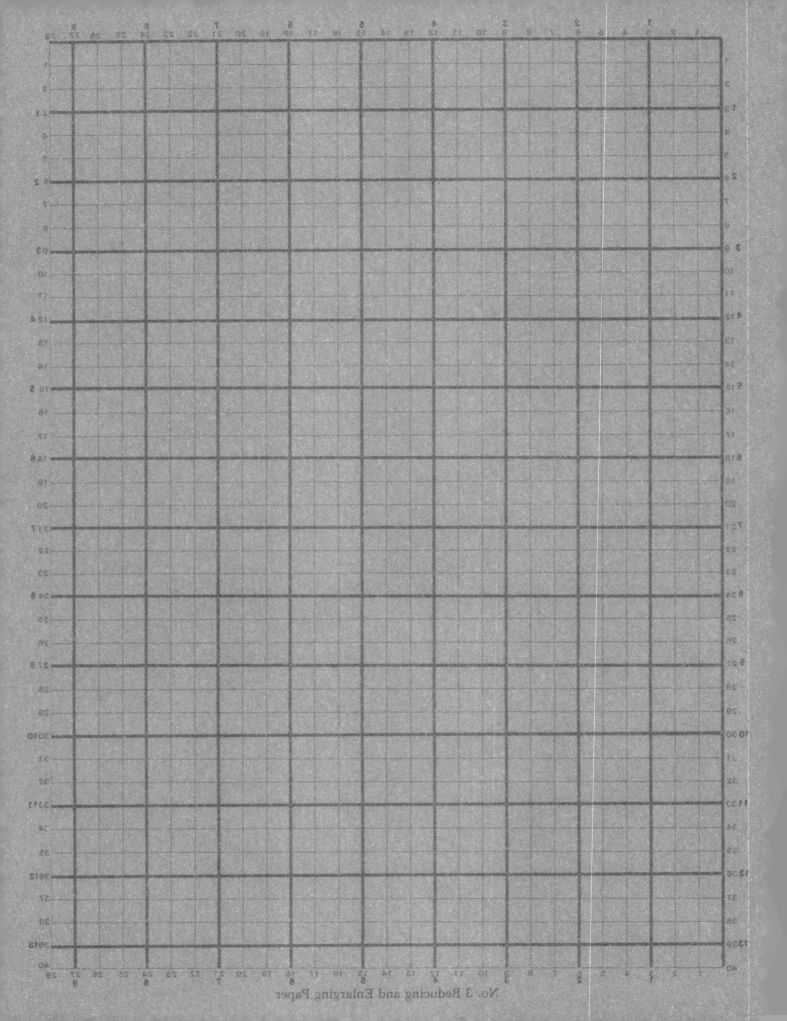

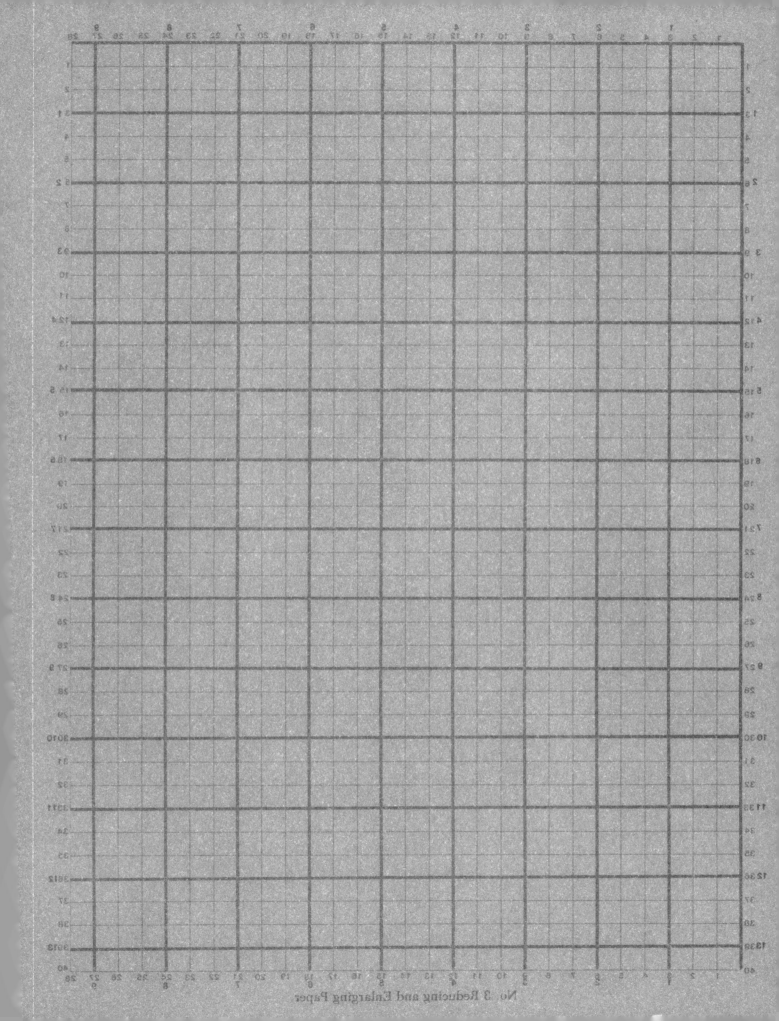

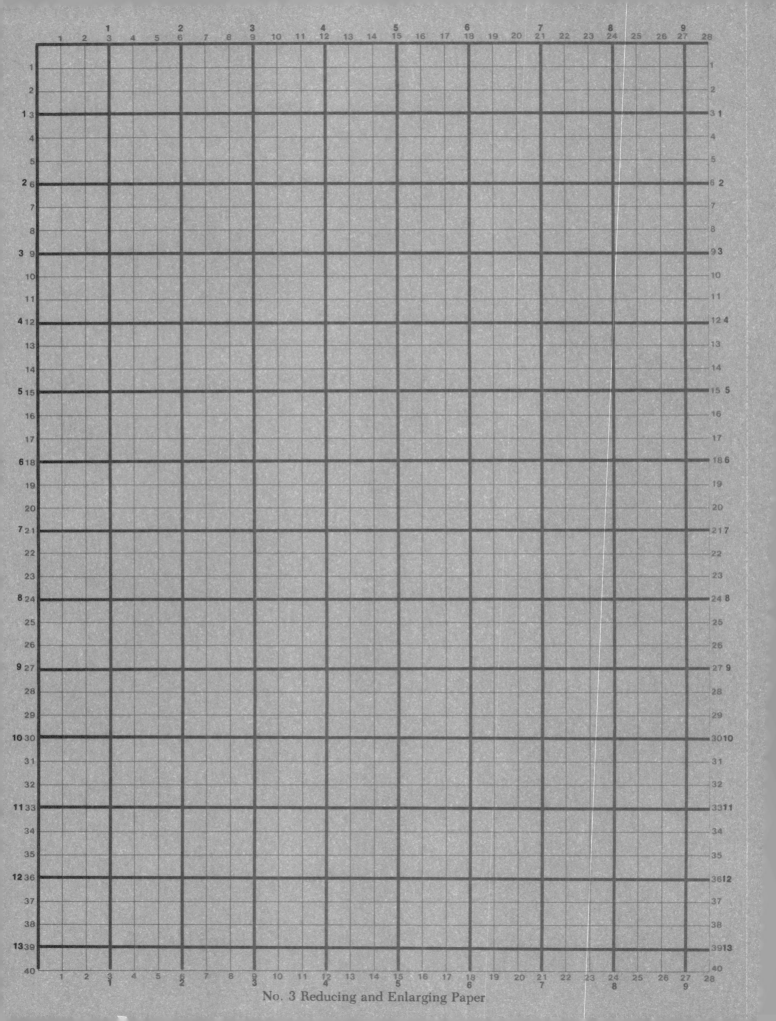

No. 3 Reducing and Enlarging Paper

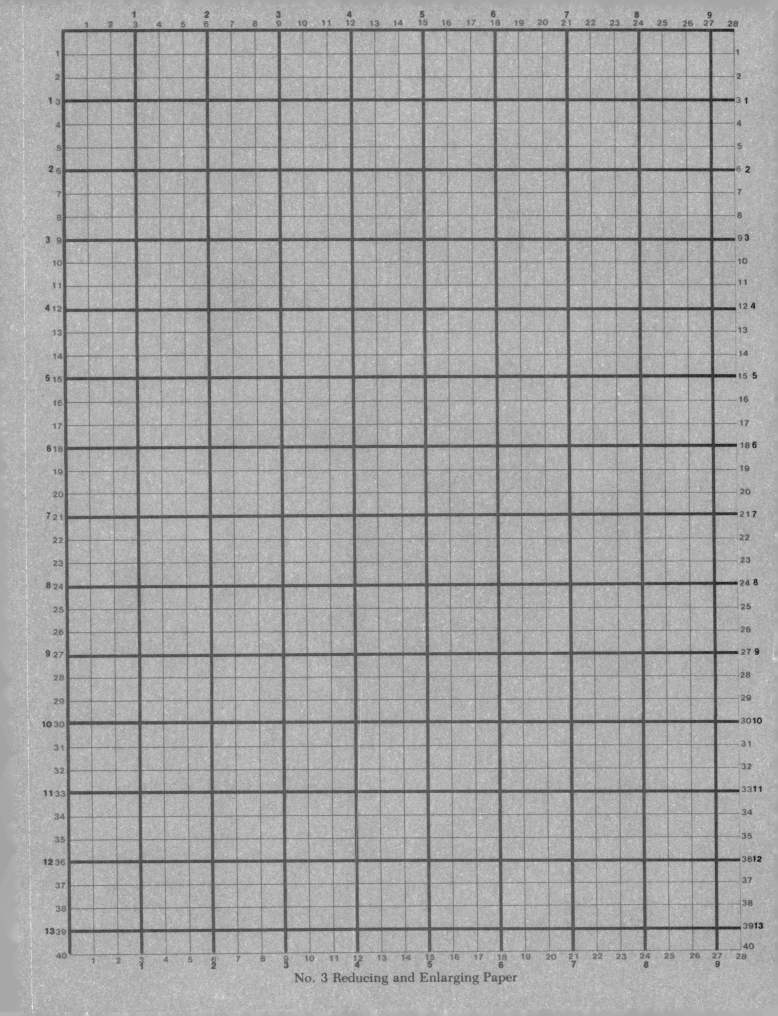

No. 3 Reducing and Enlarging Paper

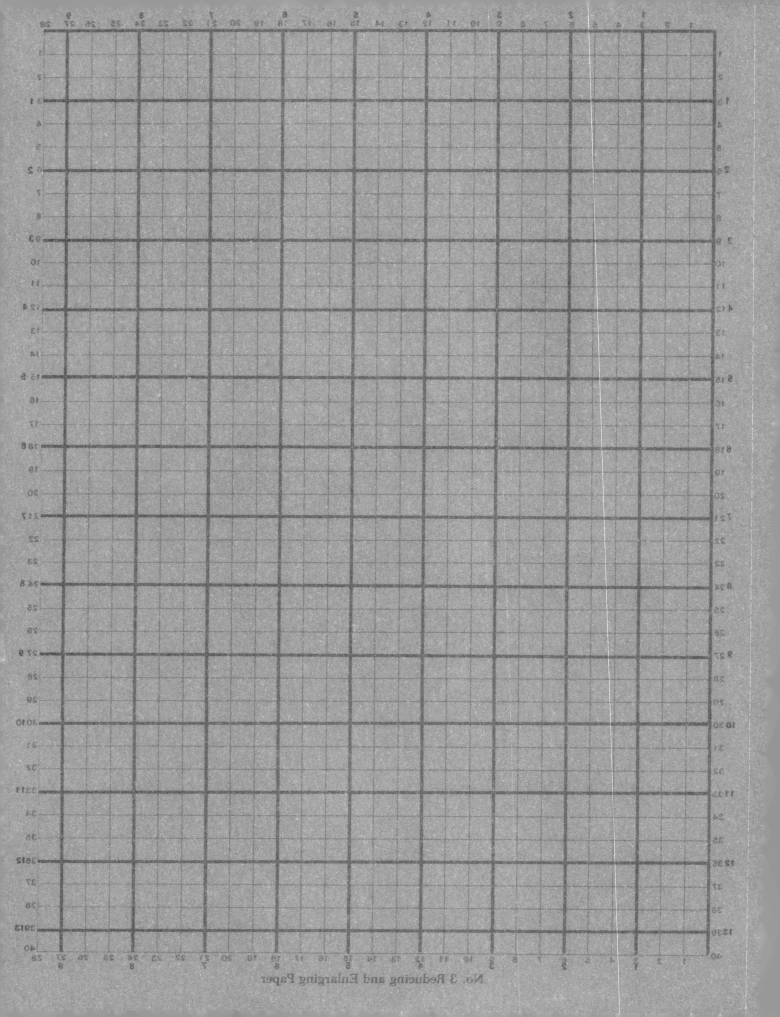

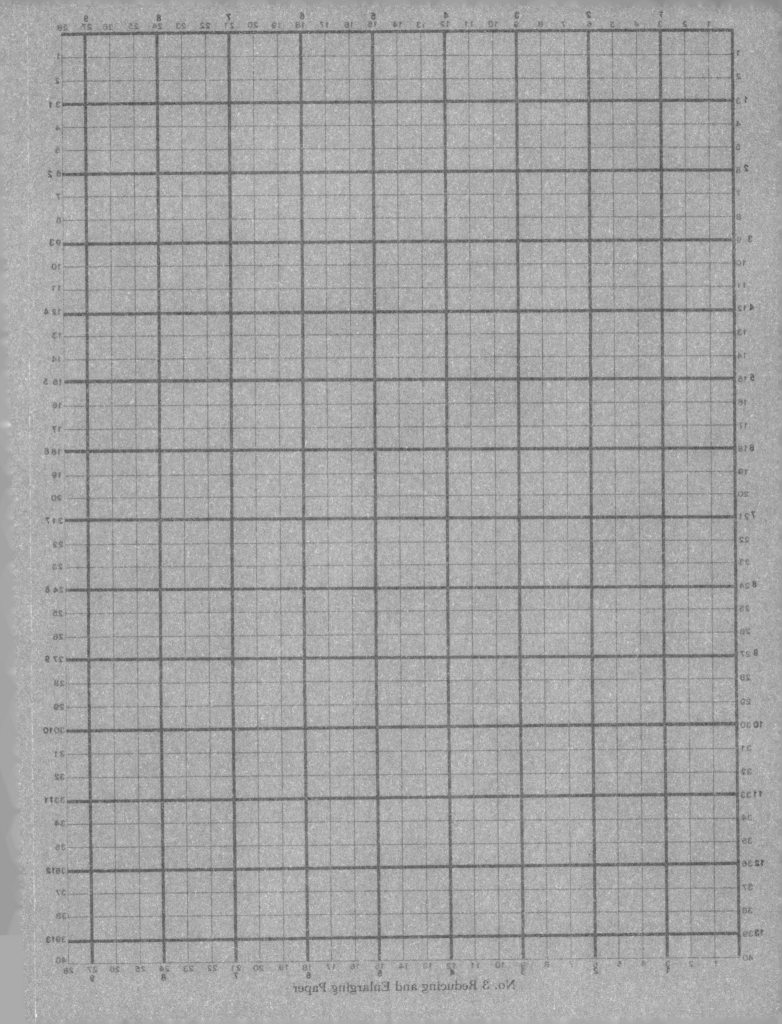

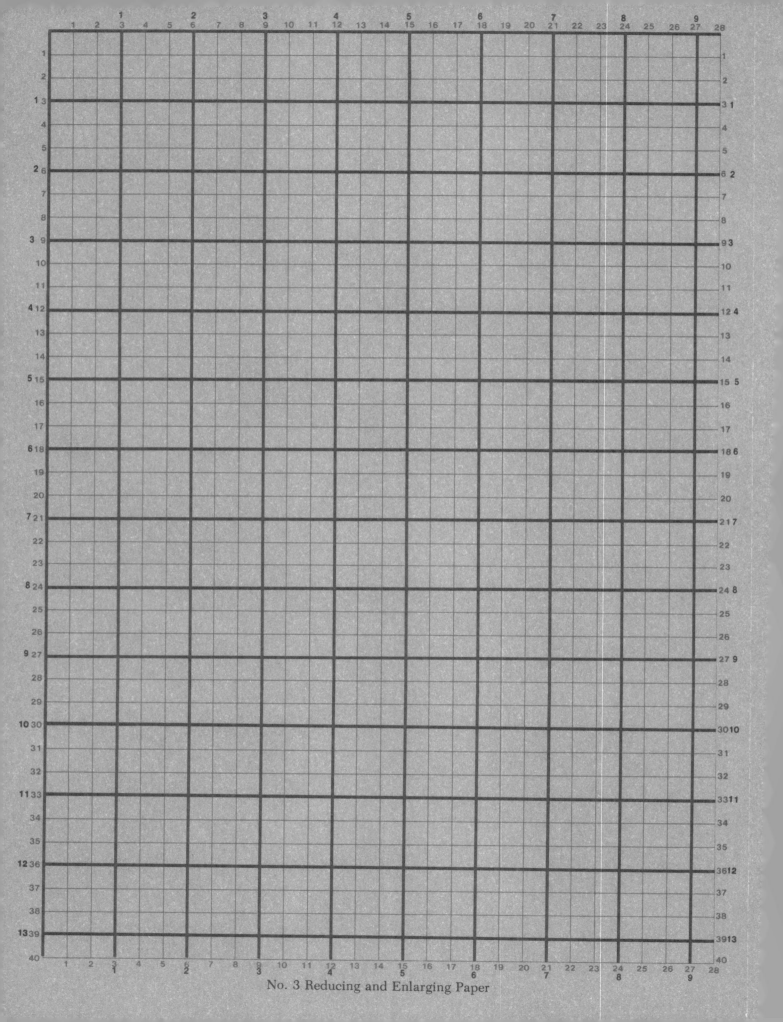

No. 3 Reducing and Enlarging Paper

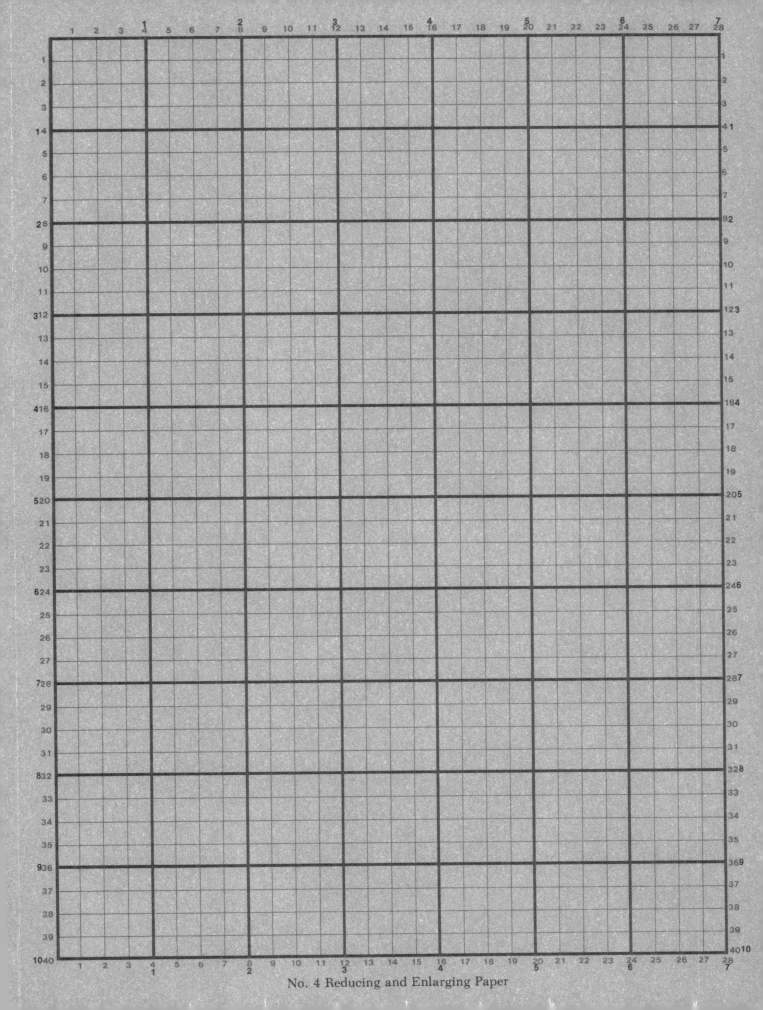

No. 4 Reducing and Enlarging Paper

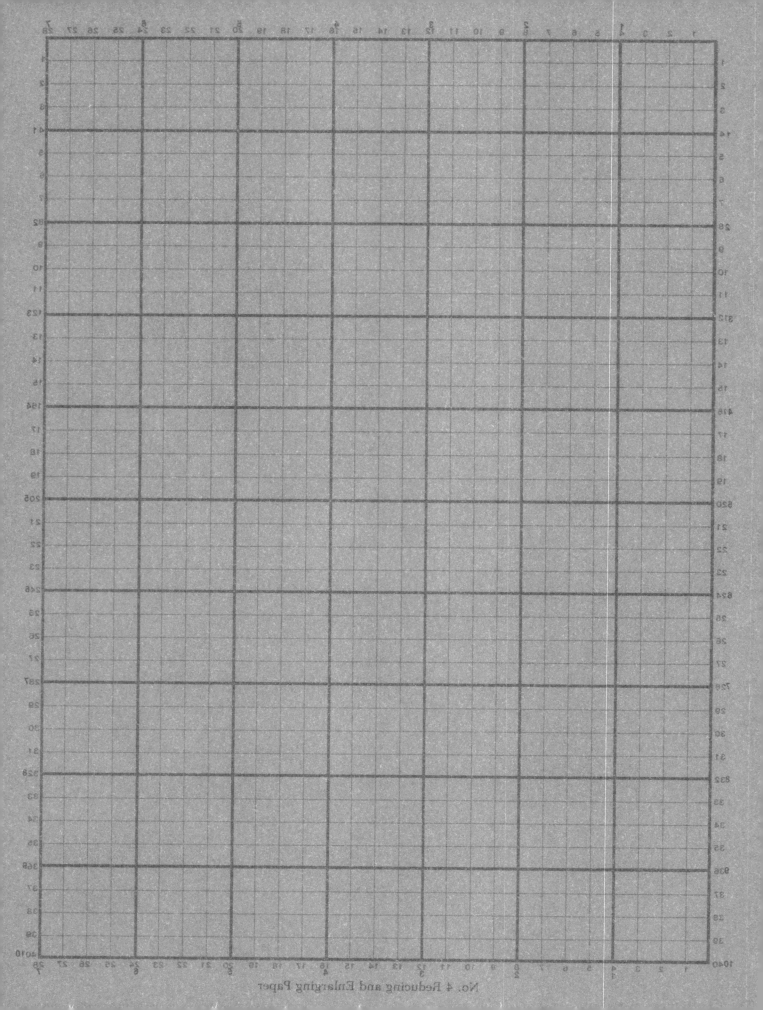

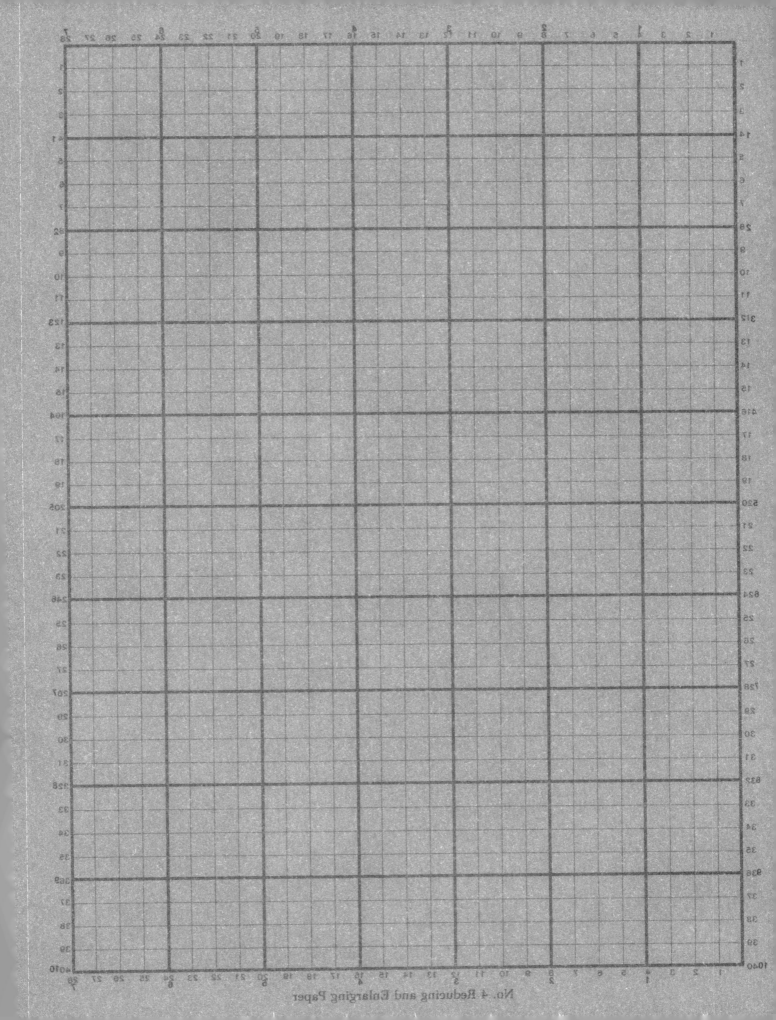

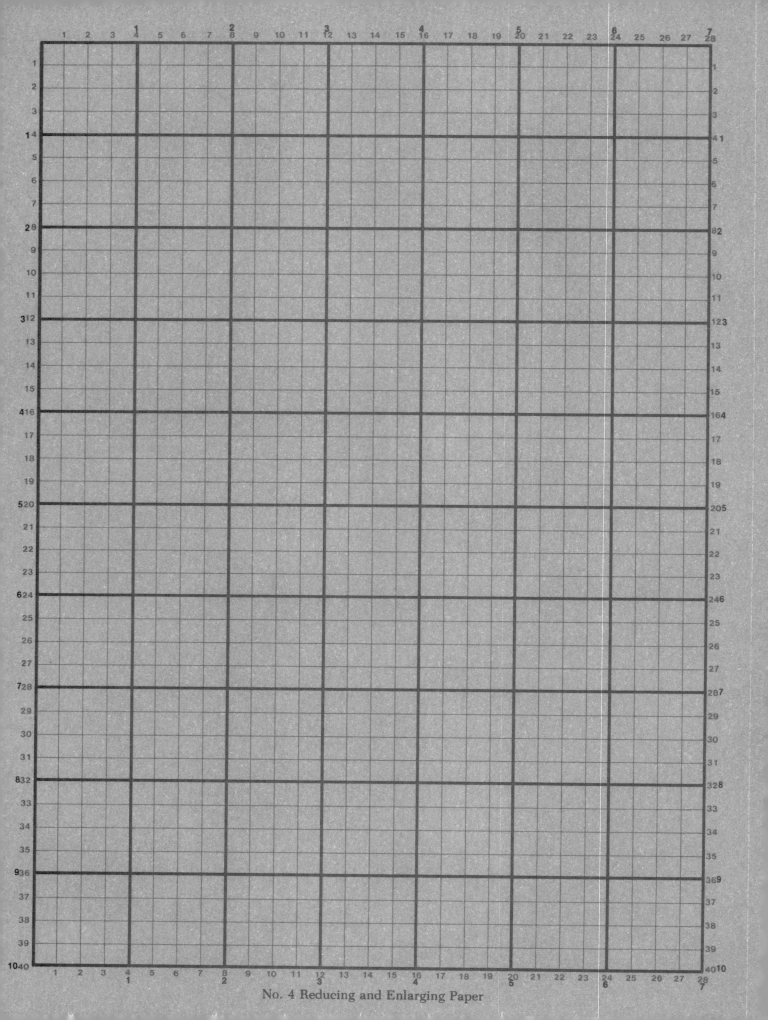

No. 4 Reducing and Enlarging Paper

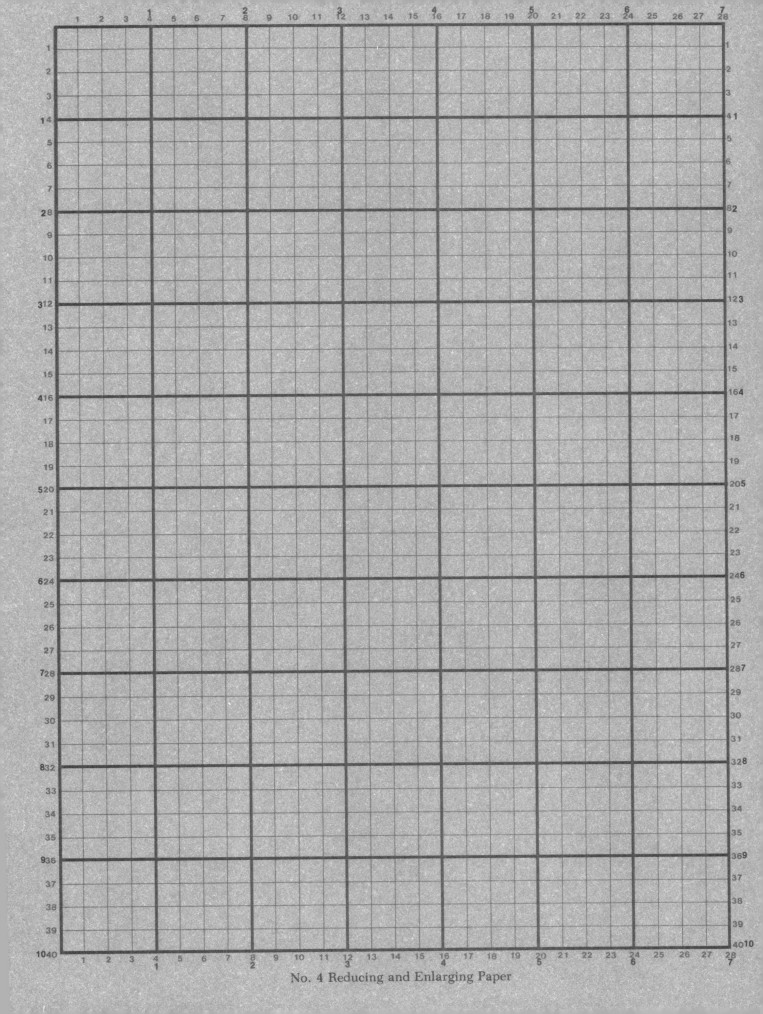

No. 4 Reducing and Enlarging Paper

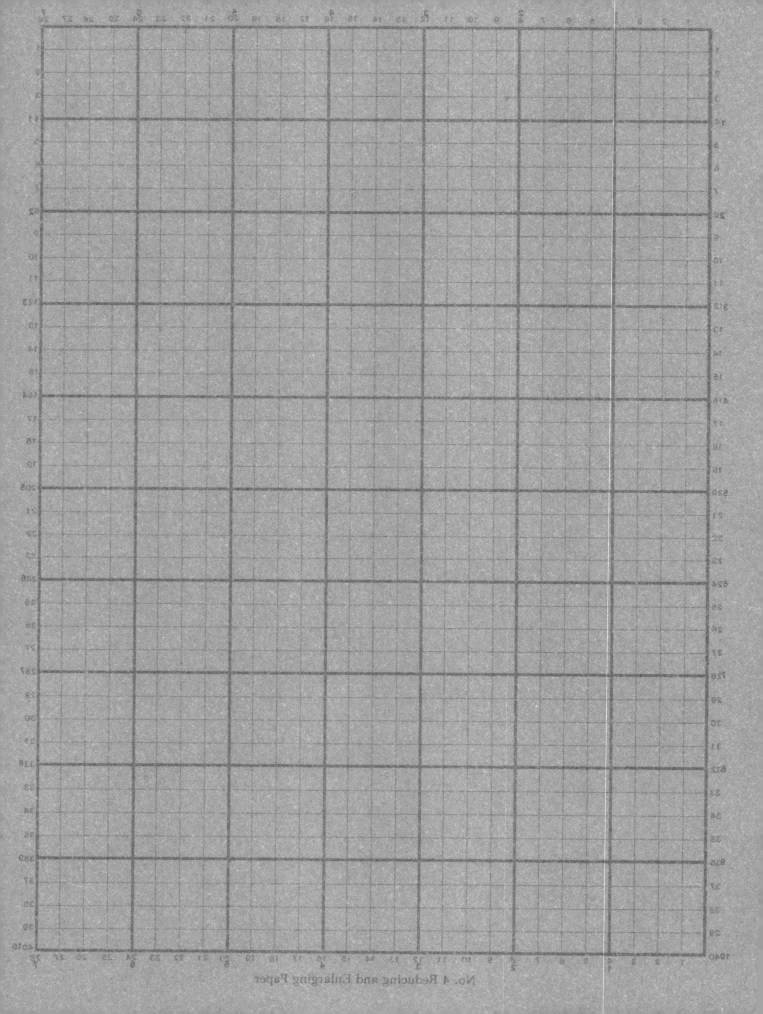

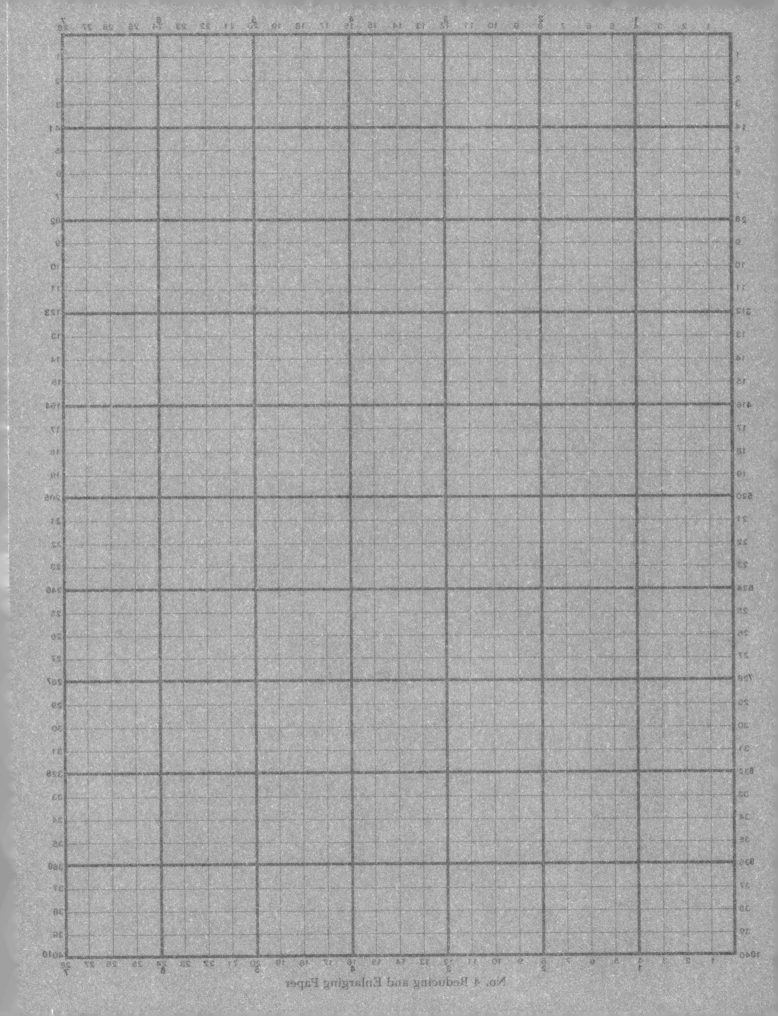

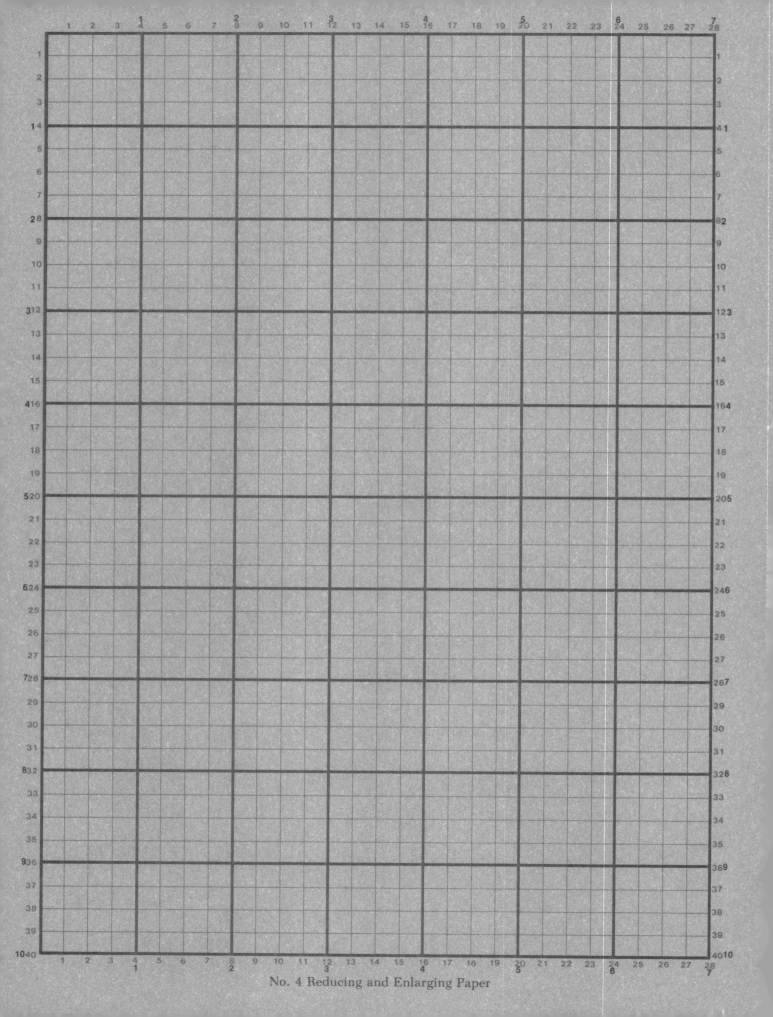

No. 4 Reducing and Enlarging Paper

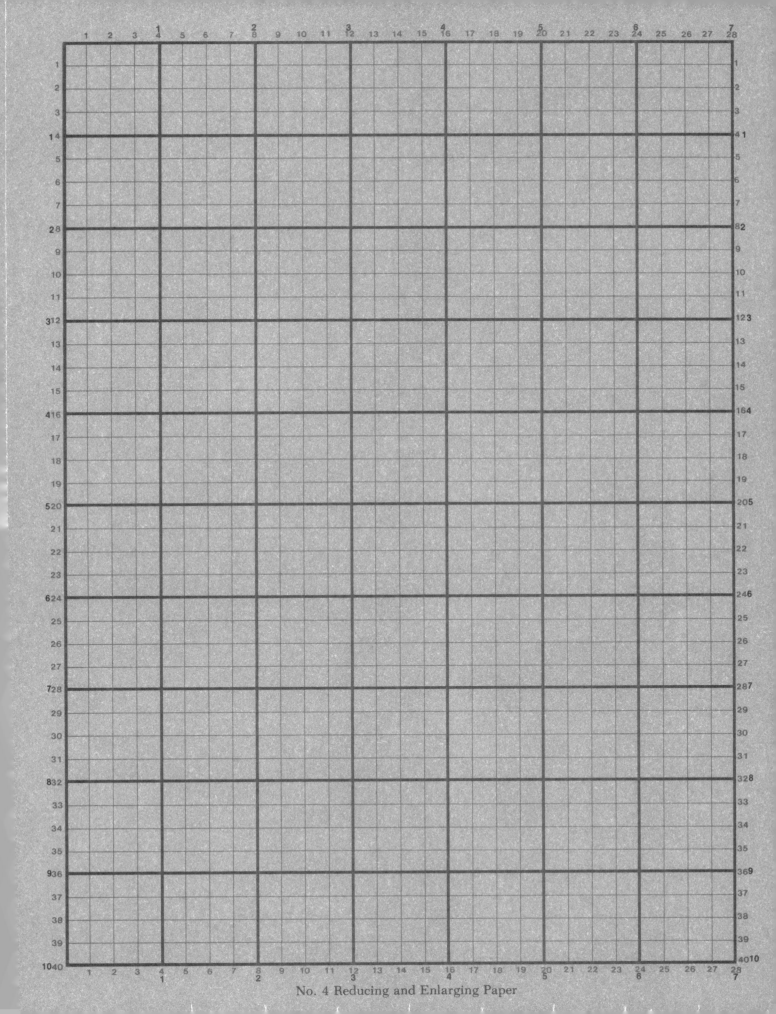

No. 4 Reducing and Enlarging Paper

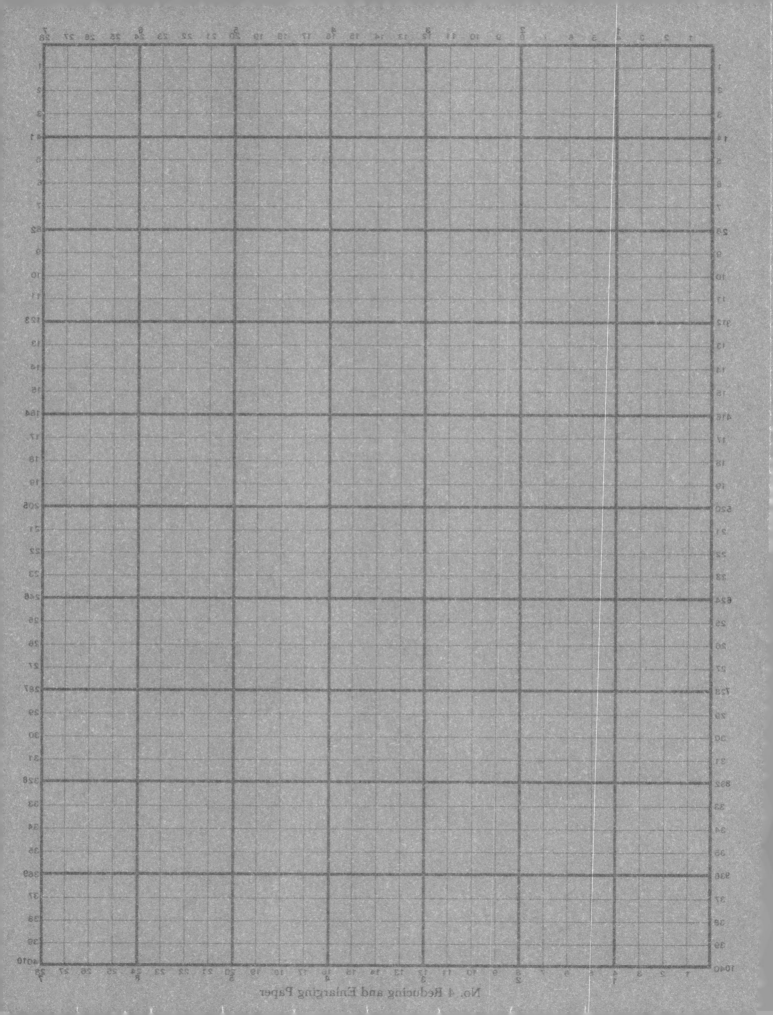

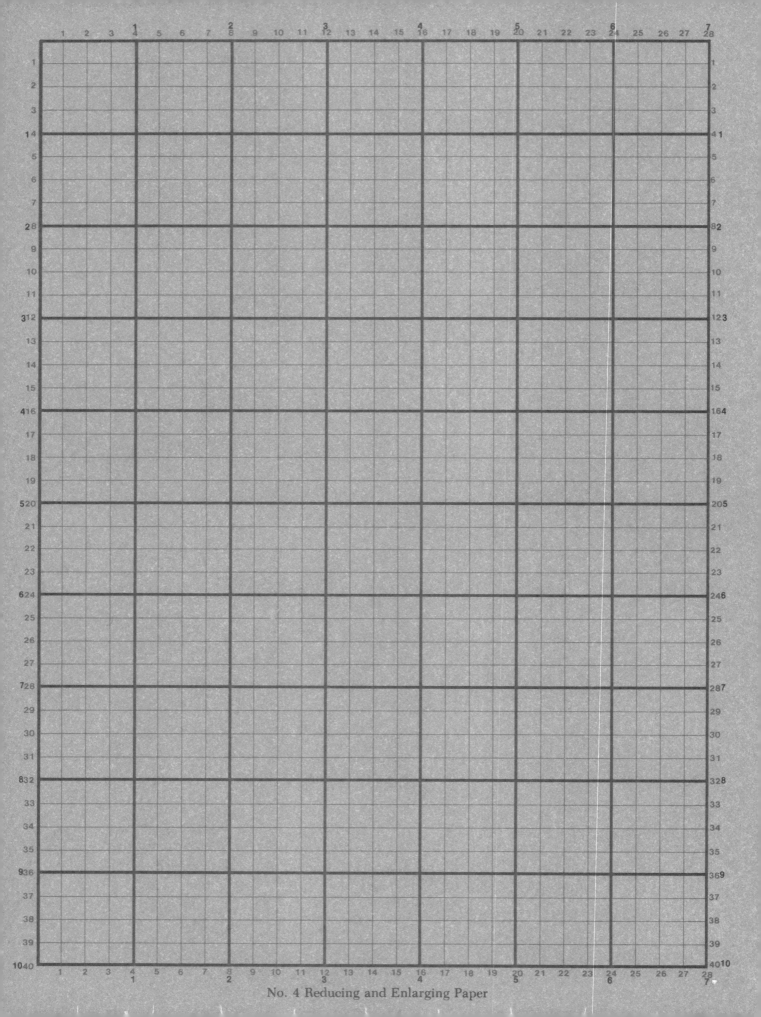

No. 4 Reducing and Enlarging Paper

Whichever method you decide to use, try to keep the design and the article you are transferring onto as flat as possible during the transfer process. Try to eliminate any shifting or movement which will render the design blurred.

Carbon Paper

This is one of the simplest and most popular transferring methods. Carbon paper will transfer designs onto wood, paper, cloth or almost any other medium you might be working in. The paper is readily available and inexpensive. Lay the craft article on a flat surface and secure it with either tape, pins or thumbtacks, or the like. If you are working with a soft material, such as fabric or paper, it is a good idea to place a piece of heavy cardboard on the flat surface; this protects the surface from scarring under the pressure while also providing the firm base necessary to produce a smooth line.

Carefully position your design on the craft article and secure the design at the four corners, using either pins, tape or thumbtacks. If the design is to be centered, use a ruler to determine the exact location.

Slip the carbon paper, color-side down, between the design and the craft article, temporarily removing one of the corner fasteners if necessary. Do not pin the carbon in place.

With a hard, even pressure trace a few lines with a tracing tool. Various tools can be used to do the actual tracing: a soft lead pencil, a stylus, a ballpoint pen which no longer has any ink, the blunt edge of a spoon, a dressmaker's tracing wheel, a knitting needle or the end of a crochet hook. Remove one corner fastener and raise one corner of the tracing and the carbon to check the impression. The desired strength of line will depend upon the craft project. If you intend to cover the line, too heavy a line may be difficult to hide; too faint a line may be hard to see. Keep in mind that the transfer may have a tendency to fade a bit in handling and so should probably be a bit on the heavy side. After adjusting the impression, trace the entire design. Remove the carbon paper and carefully remove one fastener to see whether the design is intact on the material *before removing the pattern.* Once removed it is almost impossible to re-register the pattern to the material.

Carbon paper does have a number of disadvantages that may or may not apply to your particular project. Marks made by carbon paper are permanent! Mistakes cannot be corrected, and you must be extremely careful to avoid pressing with any object—including your hands—because the pressure will create black smudges. Any unwanted lines or smudges produced by the carbon paper will be difficult to wash out of fabric or erase from wood.

Graphite Paper

Because graphite paper tends to smear less than carbon paper and is therefore cleaner to work with, it is preferred by many craft workers. It is, however, not as readily available as carbon paper. It is used in the same manner as carbon paper.

Dressmaker's Carbon

This is a special type of carbon paper with a hard, waxy finish that has been specifically designed to put markings on fabric. It will not smudge and rub off on the fabric, and the lines will wash out of most fabrics with hot or cold water. Dressmaker's carbon is available at notions, fabric, needlework and craft shops. It is used in the same manner as carbon paper.

Chalk Backing

The design must first be traced onto tracing paper. (If the design is already on one of the sheets of Reducing and Enlarging Paper, this step will not be necessary.) Turn the paper over and cover the back of the sheet with colored chalk. Use a color which will contrast with the color of your craft article.

Lay the craft article on a flat surface and secure it with tape, pins or thumbtacks. If necessary, place a piece of heavy cardboard on the flat surface to protect the surface from marring and to provide a firm padding under a soft craft article such as fabric or paper.

Carefully position your design chalk side down on the craft project and secure at the four corners using either pins, tape or thumbtacks.

With a hard lead pencil, trace a few lines. Raise one corner of the chalked design to check the impression. If the results are too faint, apply more pressure; if too heavy, less pressure. Since the chalk transfer has a tendency to fade as it is handled, the line should be on the heavy side. After determining the correct pressure, trace the entire design. Carefully remove one fastener to see whether the design is intact on the material before removing the chalked design; once removed, it will be all but impossible to re-register the design to the craft project.

The chalk-backing method works on almost any medium—paper, wood, fabric, etc.—but it produces a line that is not permanent. Just the touch of your hand will cause the chalk to start disappearing. This has the advantage of allowing for the correcting of mistakes; however, if you wish to work from the line—as in an embroidery project—you will have to retrace the line on your material before beginning to work. If you are planning to paint a design, the chalked line can be quickly covered with paint before it disappears.

Pencil Backing

This is a simple, quick method of transferring a few lines and works on the same principle as the chalk-backing method. First, put your design on a fairly thin paper, such as tracing paper or the Reducing and Enlarging Paper from this book. Turn the tracing over and cover the back of the sheet with pencil marks made with a soft lead pencil. (It is not necessary to cover the entire sheet, but be sure that the pencil marks cover all of the lines to be transferred.) Follow the instructions for making transfers with a chalk backing.

Transfers made by this method are probably the least satisfactory for craft workers. You must be extremely careful that the soft lead pencil lines on the back of the sheet cover all of the lines to be transferred. This can be time consuming if the pattern is large. The transfer made on the new material will have all of the disadvantages of the carbon-paper method without any of the advantages. The one big advantage of the pencil-backing method is that it is inexpensive, not requiring the purchase of any additional materials.

Templates

This method is especially useful when only the outline of a design is necessary or when a geometric design is going to be used over and over again. It is the method that has been used for years in patchwork quilt making.

Templates can be made from heavy cardboard, wood, plastic or any other sturdy material. The material that you use for your template will be dependent upon the number of times you plan to use it as well as the material you will use it on. A cardboard template is probably the easiest to make and works well on all media. However, the cardboard will not keep its shape indefinitely. The constant tracing around the template with even a soft lead pencil will begin to wear the edges so that by the time you have used it ten or twelve times, the pattern will have changed its shape. But if you are planning to use the template only a few times, a cardboard template is perfectly satisfactory. A wood template will retain its shape, but cutting one out will require skill with a saw. If you are going to use the template many times, the best material is plastic. You can purchase plastic sheets at quilt shops, craft shops or stationery stores, or you can use the plastic from the square milk or fruit-juice containers you buy at the supermarket. Once the container is empty, wash it carefully and then, with a pair of sharp scissors, cut it open.

Transfer the design to the material you are going to use as a template, using any of the transfer methods described above. The carbon-paper method is probably the fastest and easiest. Carefully cut out the template.

Place the template on the craft project and secure one or more ends with tape, pins or tacks. Trace around the template, using a pencil, pen, chalk or other medium which will make marks. If this line will remain as part of the pattern, make certain that the line itself will not become a problem. If it is to wash out, be certain that the medium you are using to make the line is washable.

Direct Tracing

If the material to which you are transferring the design is translucent when held to the light, such as thin fabric or paper, the transfer can be made by a direct tracing.

Tape the pattern to your light source, such as a light box or windowpane. (See page 7 for instructions on building a simple light box.) Now lay the material to which you are transferring the design over the pattern and tape the corners to keep the material from shifting during the tracing process. Trace the design using a pencil, pen or chalk. Remember that a line that must wash out should be done in a washable medium; a line which must remain should be done in a permanent medium.

Basting

This is an extremely easy method to use when transferring designs onto cloth which will be embroidered. If the design is not already on Reducing and Enlarging Paper, transfer it to a tracing paper. The basting method will destroy the design, so if you wish to retain the pattern, make an additional tracing. Pin the design in its proper position on the fabric. Outline the design with running or basting stitches through both the paper and the material. Carefully tear away the paper, leaving the design roughly outlined with basting stitches upon the fabric. Remove the basting stitches as you work the embroidery.

Pricking and Pouncing

This is a very old method that has been used for hundreds of years to transfer embroidery designs. Although it is not a simple technique, it is still extremely useful for transferring designs to thick fabric such as velvets which do not lend themselves to other transferring techniques. Traditionally a special pricking tool, which resembled a thick pin mounted into a handle, was used to make the holes, and the pouncing was done with a pouncing pad and special powdered chalk or charcoal. This method can be used today by employing materials that you will find around your own home.

If the design is not on a piece of Reducing and Enlarging Paper, trace the design onto a sheet of tracing paper. This method will destroy the design, so if you wish to retain the pattern, make another tracing of it.

After the design has been put on tracing paper, the next step is to "prick" it. Lay the design on a well-padded ironing board or a thickly folded cloth, and pin it in place. "Prick" small holes all along all lines of the design. The little holes must be "pricked" closely together, particularly where the finer and more intricate parts of the design occur; there should be approximately 15 to 25 holes per inch. A dressmaker's tracing wheel can be used for bold outlines, but when the lines of the design are very fine, the holes must be made with a very fine needle or straight pin. The holes can also be made by feeding the tracing paper through an unthreaded sewing machine, but great care must be taken not to tear the paper.

If you will need several copies of the same design, all of the copies can be made at the same time. Lay several sheets of paper together and prick through all of them at the same time in one operation. The paper must be fairly thin so that all of the copies will be clear.

After the entire design has been pricked, the wrong side of the tracing should be rubbed with a very fine sandpaper or emery paper to remove any rough edges around the holes.

Now place the material upon which the design is to be transferred on a flat surface and secure the edges with pins, tape or tacks. Lay the pricked design on the material and fasten it securely to prevent it from slipping during the pouncing. If the design is allowed to move, a "shadow" image may be reproduced on the material, and removal of the extra lines will be difficult.

"Pouncing" consists of forcing some sort of marking material into the holes. Traditionally, special "pouncing powders" were used, but various readily obtainable household products can be substituted. The important thing to remember is that the powder forced into the holes must be of a contrasting color to the material upon which the design is transferred; otherwise the outline will not appear. Powdered chalk is still the easiest material to use, and you can purchase it in some hobby and craft shops and large art-supply stores. But you can also use talcum powder, cocoa or even cinnamon. Powdered charcoal can also be used for light materials, but mix it with chalk or it will be difficult to use.

You can make your own substitute pouncing pad by taking some soft cloth or felt and rolling it into a tight bundle, about 3″ to 4″ high, which is tied around the middle. Dip the pad into the powder and dab it firmly all over the surface of the pricked paper so that the powder is forced through the little holes onto the material. When the entire design has been thoroughly rubbed over, remove the paper very carefully and gently blow away any superfluous powder collected on the material.

When the pouncing has been completed the design must be fixed upon the material before working on it, as the powder dots rub away when touched. A design which is to be painted can be outlined immediately with paint. Or the design can be retraced with a lead pencil or pen. Remember that the tracing lines must be done in a medium which will not present a problem. For instance, a line which must wash out should be done in a washable medium; a line which must remain should be done in a permanent medium.

Iron-on Transfers

There are a number of pencils and pens on the market which can make transfer patterns that can be ironed onto craft materials including fabrics and wood. The design is first traced with the transfer pen or pencil and then ironed onto the material like a printed iron-on transfer pattern. Some of these pencils and pens are easy to work with and will produce good results; others may not be suitable for your purposes. Some of these pencils and pens will produce a permanent transfer that will never wash out; others may bleed into fabric. *Always experiment before working on any project!*

All iron-on transfers will give you your design in reverse. If this is not desirable, you must first make a reverse tracing of your design before outlining with the transfer pen, pencil or ink.

You can make a homemade transfer ink by combining a teaspoon of laundry blueing with three or four tea-spoons of sugar in a little water. Mix together until the sugar disappears. Then outline your design with a thin paintbrush or a drawing pen. After the design dries, it can be ironed onto your material.

Because transfers are made with high temperatures which might melt synthetic materials, you should use a natural material for your craft project, such as a fabric with a high cotton or linen content. If you are unsure of the fibers in your material, test the ironability of it first. Before beginning any project, it is a good idea to test your iron, the fabric and the evenness of your hand pressure. Make a small test pattern and follow the directions below for transferring with a hot iron. If the ink transferred well, you can proceed; if not, you must adjust the heat, the length of time or your material, or else you must use another method of transferring your design.

Place the craft project on a flat surface, such as an ironing board, right side up. Lay the design with the printed side down onto the material and secure with pins or tacks at the corners. Place a dry iron set at about 400° (cotton or linen) on the transfer and hold down for a few seconds. Apply a firm, downward even pressure to all parts of the design. It is not a good idea to move the iron back and forth as this will tend to cause the transfer pattern to slip and blur. Carefully remove one of the fasteners and lift one side of the transfer to see whether the complete design is indicated on the material. If not, replace the fastener and repeat the process, concentrating on the area that did not transfer. Do not remove all the fasteners until you are sure that the design has been successfully transferred. Once the pattern has been unfastened, it is almost impossible to register it again. When you are satisfied that the transferring has been completed, unpin the transfer paper and peel it off.

Pressure Transfers

Several manufacturers are now producing pens which will make transfers with hand pressure rather than pressure from a hot iron. Pressure transfers work on fabric, wood, metal, glass and plastic. The Pressure-fax® Transfer Pen comes complete with pen, special transfer paper and detailed instructions on how to use the pen to make transfers for every medium. First the design is traced with the pen onto the transfer paper. Then the transfer pattern is placed on the craft project, and the transfer is rubbed with a hard surface, such as a coin or the edge of a spoon, and the design is transferred onto the craft project. When making pressure transfers, be sure to follow the manufacturer's directions for best results.

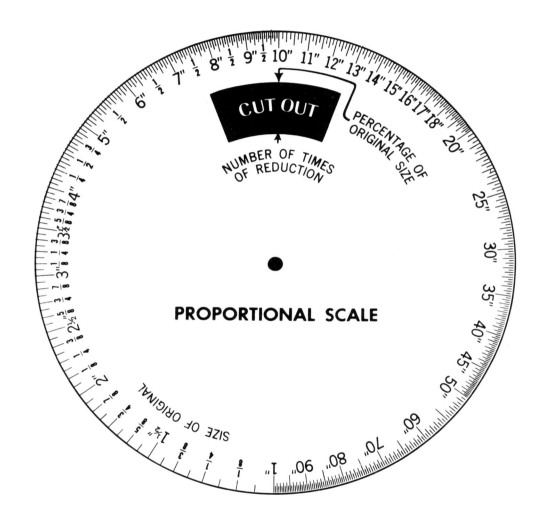

PLATE A

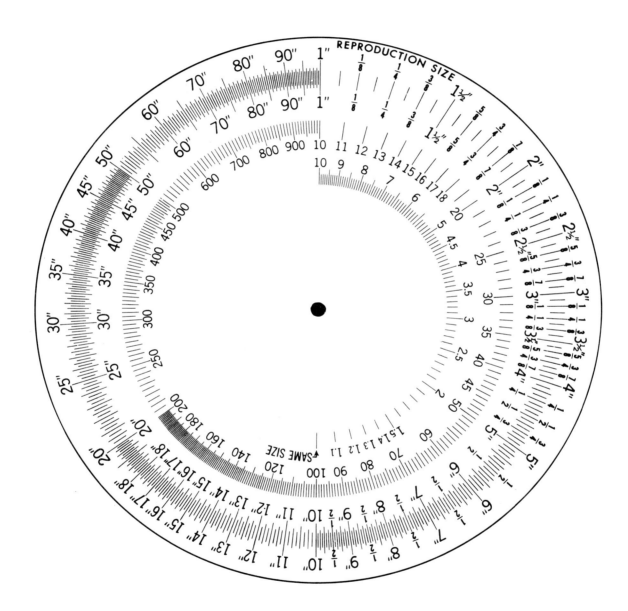

PLATE B